Adriano Shaplin

THE TRAGEDY OF
THOMAS HOBBES

The Tragedy of Thomas Hobbes was commissioned by
Massachusetts Institute of Technology and the Royal Shakespeare
Company with funds provided by Sloan Foundation.

OBERON BOOKS
LONDON

THE ROYAL SHAKESPEARE COMPANY

The Royal Shakespeare Company is one of the world's best known theatre ensembles, performing throughout the year in Stratford-upon-Avon, with regular residencies in London and Newcastle, and tours both in the UK and abroad.

Shakespeare is our in-house playwright, and central to the work of the RSC is the opportunity to investigate his influence on modern and contemporary writers. Further, our Shakespearean productions become shallow unless they relate to contemporary work which deals directly with the world we live in.

The RSC's commitment to modern classics and new work can clearly be seen in our repertoire. We will be producing more new plays over the coming seasons, and working with living writers in the Shakespeare rehearsal room. The writer's imagination will become part of the natural conversation as the ensemble investigate the plays.

We hope and believe that this reconnection of living writers with our house playwright will become one of the most mutually nourishing relationships in theatre. Shakespeare is a great teacher. His influence on contemporary writers cannot be underestimated. He knows how to marry the recognisable with the lyrical and entertainment with high art. He knows how to marry the epic with the intimate. There is a vast array of skills and stagecraft which we are inviting contemporary dramatists to plunder – just so long as they roll their sleeves up and join the actors, directors, musicians and designers in wrestling Shakespeare's beauty and vigour onto our stages.

The RSC Ensemble is generously supported by THE GATSBY CHARITABLE FOUNDATION and THE KOVNER FOUNDATION

The RSC Literary Department is generously supported by THE DRUE HEINZ TRUST

The RSC's New Work is generously supported by CHRISTOPHER SETON ABELE on behalf of THE ARGOSY FOUNDATION

The RSC is grateful for the significant support of its principal funder, Arts Council England, without which our work would not be possible. Around 50 per cent of the RSC's income is self-generated from Box Office sales, sponsorship, donations, enterprise and partnerships with other organisations.

The RSC was established in 1961, but its history stretches back to 1879 when the first permanent theatre was built in Stratford on the site of the current Royal Shakespeare and Swan Theatres.

This production of *The Tragedy of Thomas Hobbes* was first performed by the Royal Shakespeare Company at Wilton's Music Hall, London on 12 November 2008 with the following cast:

CROMWELL
Peter Shorey

LORD BROGHILL
William Beck

JOHN LILBURNE
Arsher Ali

STATLER
Leonard Fenton

WALDORF
Larrington Walker

ROBERT BOYLE
Amanda Hadingue

ROTTEN
Angus Wright

ROBERT HOOKE
Jack Laskey

THOMAS WILLIS
John Paul Connolly

JOHN WILKINS
Keir Charles

BLACK
James Garnon

THOMAS HOBBES
Stephen Boxer

JOHN WALLIS
Simon Darwen

CHRISTOPHER COX
Adrian Decosta

ISAAC NEWTON
Will Sharpe

CHARLES II
Arsher Ali

CAVALIER
Peter Shorey

All other parts played by members of the company.

This text may differ slightly from the play as performed.

DIRECTED BY
Elizabeth Freestone

DESIGNED BY
Soutra Gilmour

LIGHTING DESIGNED BY
Johanna Town

MUSIC AND SOUND BY
Adrienne Quartly

MOVEMENT BY
Anna Morrissey

COMPANY DRAMATURG
Jeanie O'Hare

COMPANY TEXT & VOICE WORK BY
Stephen Kemble

FIGHTS BY
Terry King

CREATIVE MENTOR
Janet Sonenberg

CASTING BY
Sam Jones CDG

PRODUCTION MANAGER
Pete Griffin

COSTUME SUPERVISOR
Christopher Cahill

COMPANY MANAGER
Katie Vine

COMPANY STAGE MANAGER
Alix Harvey-Thompson

DEPUTY STAGE MANAGER
Sally Hughes

ASSISTANT STAGE MANAGER
Sarah Caselton-Smith

MUSICIANS

VIOLA **Naomi Fairhurst**
CELLO **Laura Fairhurst**
SAW **Danny Schlesinger**

PRODUCTION ACKNOWLEDGMENTS

Scenery and set painting by Terry Murphy, Scenery International. Properties, costumes, armoury, wigs and make-up by RSC Workshops, Stratford-upon-Avon. Dulwich Picture Gallery and Francine Watson-Coleman. Additional costumes by Jacqui Hamer and Christopher Beales. Deputy Head of Casting Lucy Jenkins CDG. Production photographer Hugo Glendinning. Access performances provided by Mary Plackett, Ellie Packer and Julia Grundy.

The Wilton's Music Hall season is generously supported by THE WILLIAMS CHARITABLE TRUST.

One of the unspoken pleasures of working with the Histories Ensemble for two-and-a-half years was having Adriano Shaplin in my rehearsal room. This big American with an actor's projection arrived in our Clapham rehearsal rooms to give me cuts on *Richard III* that he had made on the plane. We discussed them. He also gave cuts, advice and fulsome and entertaining commentary on the following productions in the History Cycle to me, to the actors, the stage managers and everyone Front of House. He was a free-roaming provocateur for our company for two years, stirring up debate, raising the bar on just what could be said critically both in the pub and the rehearsal room.

His vigour and sheer creative magma animated the room. He gave the actors a new sense of plays and playwrights and ideas about creating character that added an extra dimension to what we did together. He also flirted outrageously with my actors and seduced them into being the mannequins on whom he draped his first draft.

He has subsequently gone on to work his play into being with a new company of actors who have been with us for the last year and *The Tragedy of Thomas Hobbes* is the result.

To lure Adriano to Stratford we promised him a two-year residency with us and Warwick University and inflicted some deep cruelty on him. We ripped him away from his cohorts The Riot Group, with whom he had lived and collaborated with for ten years. We said come and slap up against this seemingly colder fish – the English actor. There was no guarantee this would work but it was a shotgun marriage I'd gladly broker again.

Once Adriano had broken through our natural reserve the trust and creativity flowed. He has worked with an exceptional group of actors on this project, some of whom chose to join the Company particularly to work with him. We know that with the next ensemble we are already attracting actors who want to belong to a company where new roles can be created for them. It is an exciting time to be an actor who happens to know a writer at the RSC.

I hope you enjoy *The Tragedy of Thomas Hobbes*.

Michael Boyd
RSC Artistic Director

THE ROYAL SOCIETY

CELEBRATING 350 YEARS

The seventeenth century was a time when the science that we know today was really beginning to take shape. This newfound interest in the world was perhaps best recognised in the founding of the Royal Society in 1660.

The origins of the Royal Society lie in an 'invisible college' of natural philosophers which began meeting in the mid-1640s to discuss the ideas of Francis Bacon. Its official foundation date is 28 November 1660, when 12 of them met at Gresham College after a lecture by Christopher Wren and decided to found 'a Colledge for the Promoting of Physico-Mathematicall Experimentall Learning'.

The development of science since 1660 has been inextricably linked to the Royal Society. Robert Hooke was the first curator of experiments at the Royal Society and was tasked with presenting the latest scientific experiments to his peers, including Robert Boyle and Isaac Newton. Since those early days at Gresham College the leading scientists of their time have found a home at the Royal Society. Fellows have included Michael Faraday, Dorothy Hodgkin and Charles Darwin and today's Fellows include names such as Stephen Hawking and Tim Berners-Lee.

It is now almost 350 years since the founding of the Royal Society and that landmark will be celebrated in 2010. A programme of events will celebrate the contribution of science to the world around us and the input it can have to resolving problems such food shortages, energy security and climate change. Events will also mark the relationship between science and the arts.

Whether in transport, energy, entertainment or just about every other aspect of our daily lives the results of scientific endeavour are all around us. That progress owes a debt of gratitude to the scientists such as Hooke and Boyle who are featured in *The Tragedy of Thomas Hobbes*.

RSC and THE ROYAL SOCIETY

Adriano Shaplin in conversation with Simon Schaffer
Monday 24 November 2008 at 6.30pm
The Royal Society, 6-9 Carlton House Terrace, London SW1

Join playwright **Adriano Shaplin and Simon Schaffer**, Professor of History at the University of Cambridge and co-author of *Leviathan and the Air-Pump: Hobbes, Boyle and the Experimental Life*, as they discuss the germination of *The Tragedy of Thomas Hobbes* and expand on how it reflects the history of the period.

Admission free – no ticket or advance booking. Doors will open at 5.45pm. Seats allocated on a first-come-first-served basis.

THE UNIVERSITY OF
WARWICK

The CAPITAL Centre International Playwright in Residence

The CAPITAL Centre (Creativity and Performance in Teaching and Learning) is a collaboration between the University of Warwick and the Royal Shakespeare Company established to use theatre performance skills and experience to enhance student learning and to draw on University research and resources for the development of the RSC acting companies.

Adriano Shaplin is the first RSC/Warwick International Playwright in Residence. Over the past two years he has worked closely with Artistic Director Michael Boyd as an embedded writer in the rehearsal room, developing a new play for the RSC's ensemble of actors. This has allowed a unique dialogue between writer and ensemble to develop and flourish.

At Warwick, Adriano contributed to both graduate and undergraduate courses in writing for performance, working alongside the Warwick Writing Programme. In 2007 he co-directed *The Apprentice for Artists* with Peter Blegvad. This was a series of intensive masterclasses introducing aspiring writers to various forms of writing and performance.

BIOGRAPHIES

ARSHER ALI – John Lilburne/ Charles II

RSC: *The Merchant of Venice, The Taming of the Shrew.*
Trained: East 15.
Theatre: *Rafta Rafta* (National Theatre). **Television includes:** *Maxwell, Britz, Trial and Retribution.*

WILLIAM BECK – Lord Broghill

RSC: *The Merchant Of Venice, The Taming of the Shrew.*
Theatre includes: *The Agent* (Trafalgar Studios); *Festen* (Lyric); *Kes* (Royal Exchange); *They Shoot Horses Don't They?* (Edinburgh Festival).
Television includes: *Filth: The Mary Whitehouse Story, Northanger Abbey, Robin Hood, Vital Signs, Johnny and the Bomb, The Murder Room, Guardian, The Pardoner's Tale, Suspicion, Second Generation, Serious and Organised, Red Cap, Attachments.*
Film includes: *The Agent, More, More, More, Goal II, The Truth, Quicksand, Gypsy Woman, Snatch.*

STEPHEN BOXER – Thomas Hobbes

RSC: *The Taming of the Shrew, Measure For Measure* (RSC/ Barbican), *Twelfth Night* (RSC/Plymouth), *Bartholomew Fair* (RSC/Young Vic), *The Herbal Bed* (RSC/West End), *The White Devil, The General From America, Richard III, Rousseau's Tale* (RSC Fringe), *Barbarians, The Duchess of Malfi.*
Theatre includes: *The Great Highway* (Gate); *The Hypochondriac, A Chaste Maid in Cheapside* (Almeida); *Aristocrats, Power, Volpone, At Our Table, White Chameleon, The Shape of the Table, Once in a While The Odd Thing Happens* (National Theatre); *Love and Marriage* (tour); *Ten Rounds* (Tricycle); *Antarctica, Portraits* (Savoy); *Six Characters in Search of an Author, The Tempest, Bartholomew Fair* (Young Vic); *God and Stephen Hawking* (Theatre Royal Bath); *Six Degrees of Separation, Wuthering Heights, Mystery Bouffe, A Midsummer Night's Dream* (Crucible); *Oleanna* (Leicester Haymarket); *Measure For Measure* (Cheek By Jowl); *The Clearing* (Bush); *Karate Billy Comes Home* (Royal Court).
Television includes: *Doctors, Mysterious Creatures, The Quatermass Experiment, Midsomer Murders, Cherished, Life Begins, Silent Witness, Tom Brown's Schooldays, Dalziel and Pascoe, The Bill, Trial and Retribution, Absolute Power, Rosemary and Thyme, Ultimate Force, Trust, Sons and Lovers, Murphy's Law, In Deep, The Politician's Wife, Prime Suspect.*
Film includes: *Children of Men, Seven Seconds, Rabbit on the Moon, Aka, Mary Reilly, Carrington, Crossing the Border.*

KEIR CHARLES – John Wilkins

RSC: *The Merchant of Venice, The Taming of the Shrew.*

Theatre includes: *Elling* (Bush/ Trafalgar); *Pool No Water* (Lyric Hammersmith/tour); *On the Piste* (Birmingham Rep); *Incomplete and Random Acts of Kindness* (Royal Court); *Baal* (Young Vic workshop); *Romeo and Juliet* (Liverpool Playhouse); *Eye Contact* (Riverside Studios); *Keepers* (Hampstead); *Cadillac Ranch* (Soho); *Swinging with Janet* (tour); *Sunday in the Park with George* (National Theatre); *Oliver!* (tour).

Television includes: *Fear of Fanny, HG Wells: War With the World, Our Hidden Lives, Green Wing, The Bill, Dirty War, Family Business, Holby City, Ed Stone is Dead, Attachments, EastEnders, Dinotopia, Band of Brothers, Always Be Closing.*

Film includes: *High Heels and Low Lifes, Love Actually.*

Short film includes: *Sand, What Larry Says, Thank You Cori Oliver.*

Radio: *Intent to Supply.*

JOHN PAUL CONNOLLY – Thomas Willis

RSC: *The Merchant of Venice, The Taming of the Shrew.*

Trained: RADA.

Theatre includes: *Game Theory* (Traverse); *Nan, Tinker's Wedding, Shakes V Shav, A Journey to London, Double Double, Engaged, The Road to Ruin, Saint's Day, Happy Birthday Dear Alice* (Orange Tree); *Romeo and Juliet* (Ipswich); *Hamlet, The Beauty Queen of Leenane, The Communication Cord* (Basingstoke); *A Midsummer Night's Dream* (New York/London); *Romeo and Juliet* (Shakespeare's Globe); *The Playboy of the Western World* (Royal Exchange); *Neville's Island, The Three Musketeers* (York); *Observe the Sons of Ulster, Pictures of Tomorrow, She Stoops to Conquer* (Belfast); *Romeo and Juliet* (Leicester); *Twelve Angry Men, Death of a Salesman* (Westcliff). In the West End: *Juno and the Paycock, The Plough and the Stars.*

Television includes: *The Bill, Murder Rooms, The Armando Iannucci Shows, Lorna Doone, Wing and a Prayer, Birds of a Feather, Berkeley Square, The Broker's Man, Sharman, To Play the King, The Chief, You, Me and Marley.*

Radio includes: *I Can See Clearly Now, Pictures of Tomorrow, Dividing Force.*

SIMON DARWEN – John Wallis

RSC: *The Merchant of Venice, The Taming of the Shrew.*

Trained: The Webber Douglas Academy Of Dramatic Art. Awarded the Walter Johnstone Douglas Memorial Award For Classical Acting.

Theatre includes: *1 In 5* (Hampstead); *Fanny & Faggot, Present Tense* (Trafalgar Studios); *Flamingos* (Latitude); *Stars Fell All Night* (Theatre 503); *The Wonder: A Woman Keeps a Secret* (BAC); *24 Hour Plays: Ready* (Old Vic); *Nikolina* (Theatre Royal Bath); *Bedtime for Bastards* (Old Red Lion). Simon is an ensemble actor of Drywrite.

Film includes: *Morris: A Life With Bells On, A Simple Man, Howard Everyman.*

Radio includes: *Mayfly, Ready.*

ADRIAN DECOSTA – Christopher Cox

RSC: *The Merchant of Venice, The Taming of the Shrew.*

Trained: Rose Bruford.

Theatre: *Ma Vie en Rose* (Young Vic). Theatre whilst training includes: *Bellas Gate Boy* (The Barn); *The Inland Sea* (Greenwich); *Cruel and Tender, The Crucible, The Winter's Tale, The Possibilities.*

LEONARD FENTON – Statler

RSC: *The Merchant of Venice, The Taming of the Shrew, Major Barbara, Twelfth Night, London Assurance.*

Theatre includes: *Krapp's Last Tape, The Lovers* (Traverse); *Much Ado About Nothing, A Month In The Country, Don Juan* (National Theatre); *Hamlet, Arms and the Man, A Man for All Seasons* (Bristol Old Vic); *Magnificence, The Old Ones, Crete and Sergeant Pepper, The Long and the Short and the Tall, The Anarchists, Live Like Pigs, Happy Days* (English Stage Company); *Pure Gold* (Soho); *The Disputation, The Bespoke Overcoat, The Hebrew Lesson, The Square* (New End Theatre); *Saint's Day* (Orange Tree); *A Midsummer Night's Dream* (Almeida); *The Bed Before Yesterday, The Seagull* (Lyric, Shaftesbury Avenue); *Henry IV* (Arts Council Tour); *Macbeth, Twelfth Night, Much Ado About Nothing* (Ludlow Festival).

Television includes: *EastEnders, Shine on Harvey Moon, Colditz, Z Cars.*

Film includes: *The Bridge, Miracle at Midnight, Up the Creek.*

ELIZABETH FREESTONE – Director

RSC: Elizabeth directed *The Comedy of Errors* (Swan Theatre) with the Royal Welsh College of Music and Drama for the Complete Works Festival. As Assistant Director: *Speaking Like Magpies, A New Way to Please You, Believe What You Will.*

Other recent productions include: *Romeo and Juliet* (Shakespeare's Globe/UK/European tour); *Three Sisters* (Royal Welsh College of Music and Drama, Sherman Theatre Cardiff); *The Water Harvest* (Theatre 503); *Skellig* (tour); *Six Characters in Search of an Author* (Central School of Speech and Drama); *Lock The Gates* (Lyric); *Left On Church Street* (Bridewell). She was Associate Director on *The Caucasian Chalk Circle* at the National Theatre, Staff Director on *Market Boy* (National Theatre). Elizabeth was Literary Associate at Soho Theatre and has worked as an Assistant Director at the Royal Court and Hampstead. Elizabeth trained at the National Theatre Studio where she was a Director on Attachment until early 2008.

JAMES GARNON – Black

RSC: *The Merchant of Venice, The Taming of the Shrew, The Tempest, The Winter's Tale, Pericles.*

Trained: RADA.

Theatre includes: *Hamlet* (The Factory); *One Flew Over the Cuckoo's Nest* (UK tour); *The Barber of Seville* (Bristol Old Vic); *The Storm, Romeo and Juliet, Dido Queen of Carthage*

(Shakespeare's Globe); *A Midsummer Night's Dream* (New York/London); *Twelfth Night* (Shakespeare's Globe/US tour); *A Midsummer Night's Dream, The Blue Room, Les Liaisons Dangereuses* (Theatre Royal York). James is a founder member of The Factory.

Television includes: *The Brussels, Without Motive, Spilt Milk.*
Radio: *Mrs Doings.*

SOUTRA GILMOUR – Designer

Trained: Wimbledon School of Arts.
Theatre includes: *Eric's* (Liverpool Playhouse); *Piaf* (Donmar/Vaudeville); *Oxford Street, Country Music* (Royal Court); *The Lover and the Collection* (Criterion); *A Doll's House, Our Friends in the North, Rugby Moon, Son of Man* (Northern Stage); *Last Easter* (Birmingham Rep); *Angels in America* (Lyric Hammersmith); *Bad Jazz, Brief History of Helen of Troy* (ATC); *The Caretaker, The Birthday Party* (Crucible); *Petrol Jesus Nightmare #5* (Traverse Theatre/Kosovo); *Lovers and War* (Strindberg Intima Theatre, Stockholm); *Monsieur Ibrahim* (Dialogue Productions); *Hair, Electra* (Gate); *Baby Doll, Therese Raquin* (Citizen's Theatre); *Life Begins Season 04, The Mayor of Zalamea* (Liverpool Everyman); *Ghost City* (59e59, New York); *When the World Was Green* (Young Vic); *Animal* (Soho/tour); *Everyman* (Maddermarket); *Through The Leaves* (Duchess/Southwark Playhouse); *Shadow of a Boy* (National Theatre).
Opera includes: *A Better Place* (ENO); *El Cimarron* (QEH); *Anna Bolena, Don Giovanni, Cosi Fan Tutte, Mary Stuart* (English Touring Opera); *The Shops, The Birds, Trouble in Tahiti,*

Mahagonny Songspiel, Walking Not Driving (The Opera Group); *The Ruckert Lieder Project* (Streetwise Opera); *Saul, Hansel and Gretel* (Opera North); *The Marriage of Figaro* (Opera 2005).
Film includes: *The Follower, Amazing Grace.*

AMANDA HADINGUE – Robert Boyle

RSC: *The Merchant of Venice, The Taming of the Shrew.*
Trained: University of Lancaster.
Theatre includes: *Office Party* (Barbican); *The Wonderful World of Dissocia* (National Theatre of Scotland/Royal Court); *Of All the People in All the World* (Stan's Cafe); *The Birthday Show* (People Show); *Waylaid* (IOU Theatre); *Obituary Show* (Bush); *The Railway Children* (Peacock Theatre); *Live from Paradise* (Station House Opera); *The Emperor and the Nightingale* (Watermill); *How to Behave* (Hampstead); *The Silver Sword* (Nottingham Playhouse); *Great Expectations* (Unicorn Theatre); *The Fruit Has Turned to Jam* (Scarlet Theatre); *Clair De Luz* (Insomniac Productions).
Television includes: *Lead Balloon, Serves You Right.*
Film: *The Queen.*
Radio includes: *Fresh Figs at 5am, Fly by Night, Poonsch.*

TERRY KING – Fight Director

RSC: *Hamlet, A Midsummer Night's Dream, The Histories Cycle, Noughts and Crosses, Antony and Cleopatra, Julius Caesar, King John, Pericles, The Indian Boy, Merry Wives the*

Musical, *Twelfth Night, As You Like It, Gunpowder Season, The Roman Actor, The Island Princess, The Malcontent, Coriolanus, The Merry Wives of Windsor, The Rivals, Richard II, The Comedy of Errors, The Lieutenant of Inishmore, Jubilee, The Tempest, Edward III, Eastward Ho, Hamlet, Singer, Richard III, Henry V, Coriolanus, Cymbeline, Othello, Macbeth.*

Other theatre includes: *The Lord of the Rings, On an Average Day, Ragtime, Chitty Chitty Bang Bang* (West End); *Accidental Death of an Anarchist, Caligula* (Donmar); *King Lear, The Murderers, Fool For Love, Duchess of Malfi, Henry V, Edmund, Jerry Springer the Opera* (National Theatre); *Oleanna, Search and Destroy, Sore Throats* (Royal Court).

Opera includes: *Othello* (WNO); *Porgy and Bess* (Glyndebourne); *West Side Story* (York); *Carmen* (ENO).

Television includes: *Fell Tiger, A Kind of Innocence, A Fatal Inversion, The Bill, EastEnders, Measure For Measure, Casualty, The Widowing of Mrs Holroyd, Death of a Salesman.*

JACK LASKEY –
Robert Hooke

RSC: *The Merchant of Venice, The Taming of the Shrew.*

Trained: RADA.

Theatre includes: *The Masque of the Red Death* (Punchdrunk); *In Extremis, Antony and Cleopatra* (Shakespeare's Globe); *Hamlet* (Haymarket, Basingstoke/tour); *Romeo and Juliet* (Blood in the Alley Irish tour); *Biloxi Blues* (Couch Potato Productions); *Hamlet* (Old Vic); *Romeo and Juliet* (Vienna's English Theatre); *The Secret*

Garden, The Railway Children (Wolsey Theatre). Jack is a member of The Factory.

Television includes: *Heartbeat, Spilt Milk* (also co-writer).

Film: *Cellar.*

Radio: *Arcadia.*

ANNA MORRISSEY –
Movement Director

RSC: *I'll Be the Devil* (RSC/Tricycle), *Timon of Athens* (RSC/Cardboard Citizens).

Theatre and Opera includes: *Hansel and Gretel* (Opera North); *Hanover Square* (Finborough); *101 Dalmatians* (Theatre Royal, Northampton); *The Barber of Seville, Manon Lescaut* (Opera Holland Park); *Dr Faustus* (Resolution! The Place); *The Tempest, A Warwickshire Testimony, As You Like It, Macbeth* (Bridge House); *The Taming of the Shrew* (Creation Theatre Co.); *Richard III* (Cambridge Arts); *Hamlet* (Cliffords Tower, York); *The Arab-Israeli Cookbook* (Tricycle); *Human Rites* (Southwark Playhouse); *Julius Caesar* (Menier Chocolate Factory); *Tamburlaine the Great* (Rose).

Anna has worked as a practitioner within the RSC Movement Department and taught at E15, Queen Mary and Westfield and Shakespeare's Globe Education.

ADRIENNE QUARTLY –
Music and Sound Designer

Trained: Central School of Speech and Drama.

Theatre includes: *365* (National Theatre of Scotland); *Stockholm* (Frantic Assembly); *Nostalgia* (Drum Theatre, Plymouth); *Torn, An Enemy of the People, Silver Birch House*

(Arcola); *The Container* (Edinburgh Fringe Festival); *Hysteria* (London International Mime Festival); *Woyzeck* (St Ann's Warehouse, New York); *93.2FM* (Royal Court); *Hideaway* (Complicite); *Playing For Time, A Touch of the Sun* (Salisbury Playhouse); *Tejas Verdes* (Gate); *NAO, Jarman Garden* (Riverside Studios). A trained musician, she appears as cellist/writer on Piano Magic's 'Artists Rifles' and compiled 'Ballerina Magic' for Gut records. She is a Sound Design tutor for Central School of Speech and Drama, and was previously a Radio Producer for Chrysalis and Inflight Productions. More details of her work can be found at www.adriennequartly.com

ADRIANO SHAPLIN – Writer

Adriano Shaplin is a co-founder of the internationally acclaimed Riot Group and has served as the company's resident playwright since 1997. He is the author of eight plays for the company including *Why I Want to Shoot Ronald Reagan, Wreck the Airline Barrier, The Zero Yard, Victory at the Dirt Palace, Pugilist Specialist, Switch Triptych* and *Hearts of Man*. In 2004 Shaplin collaborated with Philadelphia's Pig Iron Theatre Company to create *Hell Meets Henry Halfway*, which received an OBIE award for Outstanding Production. He is a four-time recipient of the Scotsman Fringe First Award. In 2006 Adriano became the first RSC/Warwick International Playwright in Residence. He is currently collaborating with Riot Group and New Paradise Laboratories on a play entitled *Ruby Ruby Ridge*. Adriano

was born and raised in Burlington, Vermont.

WILL SHARPE –
Isaac Newton

RSC: *The Merchant of Venice, The Taming of The Shrew.*

Trained: Will is 22 years old and graduated from Cambridge University where he studied Classics and was President of Footlights.

Recent credits include: *The Wrong Door* (BBC 3); *Wham Bam* (Footlights). He is also a writer, singer-songwriter and stand up comedian.

PETER SHOREY –
Cromwell/Cavalier

RSC: *The Merchant of Venice, The Taming of the Shrew.*

Theatre includes: *Measure For Measure, Twelfth Night, The Golden Ass, Richard II, Edward II* (Shakespeare's Globe, London & USA tours). Seasons at Theatre by the Lake Keswick, Watford Palace, New Vic Stoke, Theatre Royal Northampton, Dukes Lancaster, Theatre Royal York, Salisbury Playhouse, Nottingham Playhouse, Oldham Coliseum, Mercury Theatre Colchester, Birmingham Rep, Northcott Exeter, Belgrade Coventry, Gateway Chester, Warehouse Theatre Croydon, BAC, Avon Touring, Torch Milford Haven and The Drill Hall, London.

Television includes: *Compromised Immunity, Black and White and Read All Over, Patagonia, Mr Codger, Minder, The Bill.*

Writing includes: *Jack and The Beanstalk, Babes in the Wood, Dick Whittington* (Mercury Theatre,

Colchester); *Cinderella* (The Royal, Northampton).

JOHANNA TOWN – Lighting Designer

Recent and forthcoming productions include: *Fat Pig* (Comedy Theatre); *Small Craft Warnings* (Arcola); *The Glass Menagerie* (Royal Exchange/Bath Theatre Royal tour); *Cinderella, The Secret Marriage* (Scottish Opera); *Faces in the Crowd* (Royal Court Upstairs).

Other theatre includes: *Rose* (National Theatre/Broadway); *The Overwhelming, The Permanent Way, She Stoops to Conquer* (Out of Joint/National Theatre); *Hello and Goodbye, Top Girls, Via Dolorosa, Beautiful Thing* (West End); *Feelgood, Little Malcolm* (Hampstead/West End); *My Name is Rachel Corrie* (Royal Court/West End/New York); *Guantanamo Bay* (Tricycle/West End/New York); *Arabian Nights, Our Lady of Sligo* (New York); *Shopping and F**king* (Out of Joint/West End); *The Steward of Christendom* (Out of Joint /Broadway); *Macbeth* (Out of Joint World tour/Arcola); *The Triumph of Love* (Royal Exchange); *City of Angels* (Guildhall); *To Kill a Mocking Bird* (UK tour); *Talking to Terrorists* (Out of Joint/Royal Court); *The Arsonists, Rhinoceros, My Child* (Royal Court).

Opera includes: Johanna has worked with numerous opera companies including Classical Opera, Nice Opera House, Opera 80 and Music Theatre London.

LARRINGTON WALKER – Waldorf

RSC: *The Merchant of Venice, The Taming of the Shrew*.

Theatre includes: *Jenufa* (Arcola); *Daddy Cool* (Shaftesbury Theatre/Berlin); *Ska Ba Day* (Greenwich Theatre/Talawa); *Pinocchio, Old Time Story* (Theatre Royal, Stratford East); *Playboy of the West Indies* (Tricycle Theatre/Nottingham); *Stuff Happens, The Beggar's Opera, Guys and Dolls* (National Theatre); *Blues for Mr. Charlie* (Wolsey Theatre/Tricycle); *Driving Miss Daisy* (Oldham Coliseum); *Wrong Time Right Place* (Soho Theatre Company); *Whistle Down the Wind* (tour); *The Free State* (Birmingham Rep/tour); *The Merchant of Venice* (West Yorkshire Playhouse); *Lost in the Stars* (New Sussex Opera, Brighton); *Week In Week Out* (Foco Novo/Soho Poly); *Black Man's Burden* (Riverside Studios); *One Rule, One Fine Day*; *The Wizard of Oz, White Suit Blues* (Nottingham Playhouse); *Sailing Down Everest* (Roundhouse); *Fire Angel* (Her Majesty's); *Jesus Christ Superstar* (Palace Theatre).

Television includes: *The Bill, Beck, Peak Practice, Inspector Morse, Playdays, Tecx, You and Me, Thin Air, Drums Along Balmoral Drive, Fighting Back, Dead Ahead, Moon Over Soho, Murder Rap, Black on Black, Minder, The Chinese Detective, Waterloo Sunset*.

Film includes: *Human Traffic, Lamb, Burning Illusion, Yanks*.

Radio includes: *Equiano, Whose Is The Kingdom?, Rudy's Rare Records*.

Writing includes: *Spirit of Araminta* (Courtyard Theatre, Leeds); *Busy in* the City (Roundhouse); *Blood Ties* (co-writer. Royal Opera House); *Unforgettable* (Garrick/Theatre Royal Stratford East).

ANGUS WRIGHT
– Rotten

RSC: *The Merchant of Venice, Talk of the City, Hamlet, The Theban Plays, The Dybbuk, Henry IV Parts I & II, Twelfth Night.*

Theatre includes: *War Horse, St Joan, The Seagull, A Dream Play, Stuff Happens, Measure For Measure, Three Sisters, Chips With Everything, Mother Courage* (National Theatre); *Measure For Measure* (Complicite); *Twelfth Night* (Shakespeare's Globe); *Three Sisters* (Chichester Festival); *The Importance of Being Earnest* (Nottingham Playhouse); *A Midsummer Night's Dream* (Almeida); *The Rivals, Early Morning* (National Theatre Studio); *A Mongrel's Heart, Private Lives* (Royal Lyceum, Edinburgh); *Salome* (European tour); *Too Clever By Half, Uncle Vanya* (Moscow Arts Theatre School).

Television includes: *Waking the Dead, Hotel Babylon, Casanova, Winter Solstice, Wire in the Blood, Boudica, Cambridge Spies, The Way We Live Now, The Vice, Whistleblower, Attachments, Brilliant, Dalziel and Pascoe, The Painted Lady, Duck Patrol, Soldier Soldier, Pie in the Sky, Crocodile Shoes, The Bill, Between the Lines.*

Film includes: *Bank Job, Kingdom of Heaven, Nicholas Nickleby, Dr Sleep, Charlotte Gray, Labyrinth, The Affair of the Necklace, Bridget Jones's Diary, The Lover's Prayer, RKO 281, Jilting Joe, Cutthroat Island, First Knight, Frankenstein.*

Radio: Carleton Hobbs Award 1990.

FOR THE RSC AT WILTON'S MUSIC HALL

CASTING ASSISTANT
Jim Arnold

WARDROBE MISTRESS
Valerie Atkinson

LONDON MANAGER
Corinne Beaver

HEAD OF MARKETING
Lydia Cassidy

LONDON TECHNICAL MANAGER
Julian Cree

LITERARY MANAGER
Pippa Ellis

LIGHTING TECHNICIAN
Michelle Etherington

HEAD OF PRESS
Philippa Harland

PRODUCER
Tara Hull

HEAD OF CASTING
Hannah Miller

CASTING DIRECTOR
Helena Palmer

WIGS MISTRESS
Louise Ricci

LONDON ADMINISTRATION ASSISTANT
Lauren Rubery

WIGS SWING
Jennifer Simons

ASSISTANT CASTING DIRECTOR
Janine Snape

SENIOR STAGE TECHNICIAN
Kate Stokes

SENIOR LIGHTING TECHNICIAN
Andrew Taylor

LITERARY ASSISTANT
Dan Usztan

STAGE TECHNICIAN
Robert Weatherhead

SENIOR SOUND TECHNICIAN
Sarah Weltman

MARKETING, SALES AND ADVERTISING
AKA Marketing
020 7836 4747

SUPPORT THE RSC

As a registered charity the Royal Shakespeare Company relies on public support and generosity.
There are many ways you can help the RSC including joining Shakespeare's Circle, RSC Patrons, through corporate support or by leaving a bequest.

RSC PATRONS AND SHAKESPEARE'S CIRCLE

By supporting the RSC through Shakespeare's Circle and RSC Patrons you can help us to create outstanding theatre and give as many people as possible a richer and fuller understanding of Shakespeare and theatre practice. In return you receive benefits including priority booking and invitations to exclusive supporters' events. Shakespeare's Circle membership starts at £8.50 per month.

HELP SECURE OUR FUTURE

Legacy gifts ensure that the RSC can develop and flourish in the years to come, bringing the pleasure of theatre to future generations that you yourself have enjoyed.

CORPORATE PARTNERSHIPS

The RSC has a national and internationally recognised brand, whilst retaining its unique positioning as a Warwickshire-based organisation. It tours more than any other UK-based arts organisation and has annual residencies in London and Newcastle-upon-Tyne. As such it is uniquely placed to offer corporate partnership benefits across the globe.
The Company's experienced Corporate Development team can create bespoke packages around their extensive range of classical and new work productions, education programmes and online activity. These are designed to fulfil business objectives such as building client relationships, encouraging staff retention and accessing specific segments of the RSC's audience. A prestigious programme of corporate hospitality and membership packages are also available.

For more information, please telephone **01789 403470**.

For detailed information about opportunities to support the work of the RSC, visit **www.rsc.org.uk/support**.

THE ROYAL SHAKESPEARE COMPANY

The Tragedy of THOMAS HOBBES
including the birth of empirical science in ROBERT BOYLE
and the Restoration of CHARLES II

First published in 2008 by Oberon Books Ltd
521 Caledonian Road, London N7 9RH
Tel: 020 7607 3637 / Fax: 020 7607 3629
e-mail: info@oberonbooks.com
www.oberonbooks.com

A catalogue record for this book is available from the British Library.

ISBN: 978-1-84002-888-1

Cover designed by Peter Blegvad

Printed in Great Britain by CPI Antony Rowe, Chippenham.

This play is dedicated to Janet Sonenberg, who first showed me Boyle and Hooke and planted this play, and to my father John, who holds Thomas Hobbes' corner.

Many cherished friends and trusted collaborators have made direct textual intervention in this play. In theatre, no one works alone. This play would not exist without Elizabeth Freestone, the 'Green Company', Jeanie O'Hare, Michael Boyd, The Histories Ensemble, the Warwick Dramaturgy Lab, Janet Sonenberg, Diana Henderson and the students at MIT. Equally I would like to express my thanks to the following authors whose works provided valuable background in my research of this play, particularly Stephen Inwood's *The Man Who Knew Too Much*, Lisa Jardine's *The Curious Life of Robert Hooke* and *Ingenious Pursuits*, Arnold A. Rogow's *Thomas Hobbes: Radical in the Service of Reaction*, Steven Shapin's and Simon Schaffer's *Leviathan and the Air-Pump*, Robert Hooke's *Micrografia*, Thomas Hobbes' *Leviathan* and Ted Hughes' *Shakespeare and the Goddess of Complete Being.* – AS

Characters

CROMWELL, *a protector*

LORD BROGHILL, *Roger Boyle*

JOHN LILBURNE, *a leveler*

STATLER

WALDORF

ROBERT BOYLE, *a natural philosopher*

ROTTEN, *an actor*

ROBERT HOOKE, *a mechanic*

THOMAS WILLIS, *a doctor*

JOHN WILKINS, *an astronomer*

BLACK, *an actor*

THOMAS HOBBES, *a political philosopher*

JOHN WALLIS, *a mathematician*

CHRISTOPHER COX, *a glassman*

ISAAC NEWTON, *a scientist*

CHARLES II, *a king*

CAVALIER

All other parts played by the ensemble.

The role of ROBERT BOYLE *should be played by a woman.*

Although the characters and events depicted in this play are real, the chronology and details of certain events have been changed.

1.1

Two actors, BLACK and ROTTEN appear at CROMWELL's court. Roger Boyle, LORD BROGHILL, officiates.

CROMWELL: Roger Boyle who are these painted fools?

BROGHILL: Lord Protector these are players, discovered shouting in the evening in defiance of your decree, needing to be whipped and stripped of their disguises.

ROTTEN: Merciful Protector let us explain…

CROMWELL: Burn their costumes, scar their hides, and cast them out. Next!

BLACK and ROTTEN are dragged out.

BROGHILL: One Thomas Hobbes requesting safe return from exile and permission to publish in England.

THOMAS HOBBES stands forward clutching his book.

HOBBES: Strong Protector a thousand thanks for this Peace you bring to my native land!

CROMWELL: Enjoy your stay. Who is next?

HOBBES enters England.
JOHN LILBURNE is brought on in shackles.

BROGHILL: John Lilburne, charged again with seditious publication.

CROMWELL: Prithee Speak Leveler, answer this charge, let us be satisfied by thy confession.

LILBURNE: I must give thanks to our Lord Protector, Peace be upon him,
For his inquiry here, to the Free-born cause. A cause shared by all free-born men under God in England. A cause you men here have plainly abandoned. For in the beginning—

CROMWELL: No sermons!

LILBURNE: The Earth Was to be a common treasury!

BROGHILL: No sermons John. Answer the charge.

LILBURNE: I will speak no more lest I be given freedom to speak freely and fully of my mind and not bear censure.

BROGHILL: Speak freely and fully in answer to our question brother or hold your peace.

CROMWELL: Answer your Protector!

LILBURNE: I, John Lilburne, am an Englishmen, born, bred, and brought up
In England. I am governed by her laws, and her limitations.
In these I have gloried and I have suffered much,
But now I suffer to wonder *who* are these men
That summon me with soldiers and pretend my late offenses?
Who grants them the power to pose question and hold me?
And brandish their army against me in the land I were born?
I spit on any question or quarter you pose!

BROGHILL: John Lilburne answer did you make these pamphlets.

LILBURNE: Proud Protector, I fought for you. The reason was: I never saw in any Bible any law stating one branch of mankind should rule over another. Brother we know this. So it were noble to depose the king, but sheer terror to chop his block! See how, even now, this Protector perverts and usurps our revolution, lending tyranny a new head indistinguishable from the one we off'ed.

BROGHILL: Silence his contempting mouth, if it refuses to answer, clap him up.

LILBURNE: I say indistinguishable, but doesn't brother Cromwell's head make a more sinister sight indeed? Woe for England if his New Model Army dispatch, sailing us to Irish Land, now, to slay Irish! This court is a body falsely assembled, with a rotten head, peace be upon it, right at the top!

CROMWELL: Clap him up.

LILBURNE is yanked and fights, displaying super-strength.

LILBURNE: You will have me clapped in irons, so ahead with the clapping, but Gentlemen, I bid you stick me in one of England's civil jails, where the law is known, and not in those garrisoned forts where your loyal soldiers may be commanded to execute any man or be hanged. Clap me in a proper jail, or try, with your pretended charges, I dare you. For if I am Put in your Fort I do solemnly Swear before the Eternal God in Heaven I Will Fire and Burn It to the Ground for God and Pray my Martyred Heart be Closed in among the Ashes and Flame. LEEEEEEVEL IT! LEEEEVEL IT TO THE GROUND!

LILBURNE dragged out.

CROMWELL: What seditious vanity manifest in a single miserable man, thinking the End of King is the Rise of him—stupid thing, break him in pieces. Break all traitors. If you do not break them, they will break you, and bring all this blood shed in war back upon your heads. Thus rendering you unto England to be the most contemptiblest generation of weak, silly-spirited, low-hearted men ever to govern and lose ground to Fanatics. Sirs you are necessitated to break them in pieces.

TRANSITION

STATLER: The bright side in being broke to pieces is the peaceful Kingdom of Heaven you get to see straight after.

WALDORF: You'll only see it if your head finds the way. Which is hard if you're in parts. My legs might dash up to heaven and in haste kick my head down to hell.

STATLER: Surely the Spirit re-forms Whole.

WALDORF: No one knows for certain.

1.2

ROBERT BOYLE and ROTTEN kiss down a dark street. ROTTEN is dressed as a woman.

BOYLE: Was this a sin?

ROTTEN: You tell me.

BOYLE: This was a sin.

ROTTEN: You know it was.

BOYLE: Why stand here and invent this sin I never saw before?

ROTTEN: Stages are bare, entertainment scarce and all.

BOYLE: You charade in the street.

ROTTEN: He closed the brothels too.

BOYLE: Are men so fallen away from the Church?
    What makes men turn from the bosom of the Church to another breast
    And make up a faith for themselves alone?
    Turn each into the other's ear to drown out God
    With words, sweet lies, whatever curses they muster.

ROTTEN: Say you took me for a Natural woman in your mind to lessen the sin.
    Two shillings.

BOYLE: You take payment?

ROTTEN: What you think? I swap these frillies for an apron to make my
    honest living?

BOYLE: I have only just arrived in this city. I am lost, tonight, alone.
    And you here wait in the shadows to tempt me.

ROTTEN: These are nice shadows no?

BOYLE: In the darkest part of my heart.

ROTTEN: Say you left it at home, the whole heart and its dark parts, you didn't
    bring it.

BOYLE: Here I am mocked by a sinner.

ROTTEN: Call it a mocking still two shillings.

BOYLE: And so I stand a sinner with him. God sees me.
    But where was His hand to snatch away my heart?

ROTTEN: Bishop be practical.

BOYLE: I am no Bishop.

ROTTEN: Are you the only sinner God sees?

I had five others like you tonight and none of them struck dead.
They walked straight out of these shadows and none struck dead.

BOYLE: Let us make some other arrangement.

ROTTEN: Just pay or I'll crack you how about that?

BOYLE: If I pay for this sin it can never be washed away.

ROTTEN: Wash and it will be washed away.

BOYLE: Bid me help you commit this sin no more.

ROTTEN: I commit this sin for a job Bishop and for bread until things get
better.

BOYLE: Take my purse, not for that shadowy thing.
But toward a future in Christian service.

ROTTEN: Have your heavy purse back. I only want the two.
No future in Christian service.

BOYLE: I have a house with many rooms, and room for you. Laboratory.
Shining wide space. Steady work to wait on me, in a quiet proper suite. You
speak well. A capable thing, and no flatterer. Become a gentlemen, attend,
run errands, in these streets you know. Wear my coat. Dress better. Come, my
name is Robert Boyle.

ROTTEN: I come for my shillings.

Exeunt.

1.3

*A coffeehouse open-mic for the New Science, run by the Invisible Group. Alchemists,
astrologers, chemists, hobbyists, coffeehouse philosophers, shaky caffeine junkies, street corner
pundits and proselytizers are gathered around.*

STATLER: This is the stuff of stuff, come and see.

WALDORF: Boredom.

STATLER: It is some thing not politics called New Philosophy.

WALDORF: New is always bad.

STATLER: They talk about the ways of the blood in the veins, with charts and maps, and mix matters to make hellfire, you'll love it. Here is where they say the earth revolves around the sun.

WALDORF: Everybody thinks that now.

STATLER: Not everybody.

WALDORF: Everybody I know.

STATLER: But here, you'll be admired to think it.

WALDORF: Shit on that.

STATLER: Open your mind.

WALDORF: This is just a new clergy breed hissing over invisible notions.

STATLER: Maybe you're just too thick to understand it.

WALDORF: Can any of these conjurors—

STATLER: Philosophers!

WALDORF: So-called—talk politics? Ha? Is this topic within their micro-Scope?

An old Alchemist named GEOF stands to speak, shaking. Others assembled ignore him. There is some coughing.

GEOF: Look now, See here Gentlmen.
　　I see here we are waiting for our first Sayer to arrive.

WILKINS: Anatomy will be first Geof, just a moment.

GEOF: And as we share these few moments together,
　　I wish to address myself to all of you regarding some matters of a most Traditional nature.

WILLIS: Geof please sit. One moment.

GEOF: Oh Nothing so, shall we say, dazzling,
　　As is to be expected of the esteemed members of the experimental community— But, Nonetheless, Perhaps, of some pressing interest or passing interest to the many supposed men of intelligence gathered here. And

GEOF is pelted with a few jeers and wads of paper.

As many of you supposed men of intelligence have only just recently, just these weeks past, elected to decline my pamphlets at the door, where I did pass them once, and for whatever reason I cannot begin to guess, I now feel I have little choice, but to read my findings Aloud, Now, in the few precious moments we share here, prior to this mornings Most anticipated—fine with you sure it 'tis— Ahem!

WALLIS: Geof…

GEOF: 'Menstrual Witchcraft…'

COX: What are you on about man? You read that bloody thing last week.

GEOF: My exegesis on Menstrual Witchcraft?

COX: Last week dude. You're supposed to do an experiment.

WILLIS: Thanks Geof, here is my mechanic.

ROBERT HOOKE enters with a large dog, a bellows, some tools, and a detailed drawing of lungs.

ROBERT BOYLE and ROTTEN enter aside.

ROTTEN: Who runs this show?

BOYLE: John Wilkins is the secretary, but his face is unknown to me. There is the boy.

WILLIS: Gentlemen, young Robert.

ROBERT HOOKE takes the stage to mild applause.

HOOKE: By way of experimental demonstration and on behalf of good Doctor Thom Willis—

WILLIS: Ahem.

HOOKE: —I, Hooke, your steady mechanic, shall demonstrate out the good doctor's most recent anatomical theories in the theatre of respiration and lungs.

Pause.

Listen. We breathe. The dog breathes. Flexing.

This action of the lungs can be observed in most terrestrial animals,
Moving their lungs with the Aire.
And a Man cannot live more than a Few Minutes—
A little time—
Without Breathing in the Aire.
And leaving aside tales of Islanders that swim and hunt for hours—
Much time—
Breathing under the water like fish,
To which we have no witnesses—No witnesses?

ALL: No. None.

HOOKE: So we agree Man breathes in the Aire to Live,
     So God must put Aire there, to Breathe.

BOYLE: (*Aside to ROTTEN.*) A plain speaker with little bluster.

ROTTEN: (*Aside.*) He's deformed.

HOOKE: But what is Aire?
     Here Doctor Thom makes a cunning hypothesis:

ROTTEN: (*Aside.*) Sounds like some rude act.

WILLIS: That a Rarer part of Aire does Mix with the Blood in the Lungs
     By our Own Action of Respiration.

HOOKE: My experiment, tests this theory.

BOYLE: (*Aside to ROTTEN.*) See those tools. His hands are blessed.

ROTTEN: (*Aside.*) How come he gets to stand on a little stage?

HOOKE: So Upon affixing this device, I—
     This device Gentlemen my own design where I embellished a common
     bellows fitted with a second bladder to manage liquid in tandem would no
     doubt prove useful to any Doctors, Apothecaries Special Butchers, or diverse
     hobbyists could use one
     See me after for special orders—
     So Upon affixing my device, I, shall Dissect the Dog Living,
     Exposing the thorax thus, then blow Aire into its lungs to sustain its life,
     Now, who would like to assist me in subduing the animal?

Every hand in the room goes up. CHRISTOPHER COX is selected.

STATLER: There's your son. Doesn't he look fine and grown?

WALDORF: He's supposed to help me at my shop. Not be volunteering at these idle trifles.

BOYLE: (*Aside to ROTTEN.*) I must depart before the dog docs, as I cannot bear dissection at all. Find Wilkins among these men. Negotiate for the boy, on my behalf. Promise future patronage. I have long supplied them with funds, they know my name, but use a sharp tongue just the same. (*Exit.*)

HOOKE: This dog will be a martyr for knowledge, Gentlemen, hold him tight!

DOG: Yelp!

ROTTEN sidles up.

ROTTEN: I carry a message for the Secretary here, John Wilkins; who is he?

WILKINS: I am he.

ROTTEN: The message I bear is from your loving patron,
The Honorable Robert Boyle.

ROTTEN and WILKINS stand aside.

WILKINS: Robert Boyle is a man I most admire,
Though we never see his face. A longed-for and generous patron.
I imagine him busy at Bishopsgate praying for peace.

HOOKE: Hold while I make the incision!

WILKINS: Will we meet him?
We'll soon have rooms at Gresham for conducting science,
And servants at our disposal, whatever thing the Virtuoso needs.

ROTTEN: The boy there, for a start.

WILKINS: Young Hooke?

HOOKE: I spot the passage to the lungs! Wipe the blood!

ROTTEN: Boyle has heard tale of him,
Rumored to be the most skilled mechanic in your stable,
Now my eyes have spotted this little performer, we like him.
Moreover Boyle won't be needing your rooms. He has his own lab.

These surroundings, no doubt, would be a touch too rough for my master.
He is accustomed to silence when he practices science,
Not this zealous din.

DOG: Yelp!

WILKINS: That boy is taken. He is servitor to Dr. Willis.
And mightily relied on, by All in our group.
Would Boyle not consent to share Hooke's hands?

ROTTEN: No no sharing. Speak to Good Doctor Thom,
Bid him make arrangement to replace the boy.
Now I must depart before the Dog does,
As I cannot bear dissection at all. (*Exit.*)

WILKINS: Carry my blessings to the Virtuoso.

HOOKE: (*About dog.*) With my device the motion of the lungs is commanded!
Is the dog living? No it is martyred.

WALDORF: Call this philosophy? More like Cooking with Early Man, in the garden of Eden I mean.

STATLER: Secret heathen. These are marvelous pious gentlemen that believe in Creation, seeking to peep on it.

WALDORF: To peep on it or slaughter it I suppose is a worthless distinction in this room. What happens to the dog?

STATLER: Pay attention! This is early days of a new dimension,
These men will save us from ignorance, which,
In future, we'll have No more of.

WALDORF: Sure we won't, I'm going to the coffee spot

STATLER: To see your man Hobbes, that wailing peacock.

WALDORF: He's a real philosopher, take note.

STATLER: He's a Quote Real philosopher Unquote.

Exeunt.

1.4

A street in London.

BLACK: (*Solo.*) See this pamphlet in my hand?
    Is this what comes with Progress?
    Theatre is dead.
    King is chopped and abolished in a basket,
    So all Pomp and Mirth are flown away,
    From this barren land, exchanged instead for
    Dire, Vicious, grey-hot Politic—
    Which in truth I cannot bear—
    Or whomsoever's new law of motion
    Is but a farting sound, or
    Enumerating thy neighbors
    Obvious Atheism is now our soul vernacular.
    My former job in clowning is closed.
    My ambition to be a stage poet, canceled.
    Both sides of my life real and
    Imagined are crushed.
    Thank Diana I can write
    And make some coin transcribing palsied political prose
    My clown friend Rotten can't write a word
    So's whoring, poor fox, at his age, for coin.
    Venus watch my back! But if the muse won't
    Watch my back, I'll turn to Mars,
    And lend my skills calligraphic to a War of Words.
    See I am attached to a very sinewy and robust old
    Warrior, with a stammering hand,
    That lately plays the bear in winter,
    I'll wake him; and see what scribbling work I can Stir up
    Presenting to a certain man—

WALDORF: There sits Thomas Hobbes.

BLACK: These late pamphlets lettered against him. (*Exit.*)

A London coffee house. THOMAS HOBBES sits in one corner. There is a smattering of other patrons all reading newspapers and pamphlets.

WALDORF: A Learned Man of Philosophy!

STATLER: So sits grumbling alone.

WALDORF: Well such is the business of important men, men with much
    Knowledge in many areas.

STATLER: Much Knowledge and plenty Opinion where Knowledge he
    does lack.

WALDORF: Well there you show your ignorance because Mr. Hobbes doesn't
    deal in Opinions.

STATLER: Only his own.

WALDORF: He doesn't have time for them.

BLACK enters with pamphlets. WALDORF orders a coffee for HOBBES.

HOBBES: (*To BLACK.*) Where in hell have you been, man? I'm dying for a pint.
    Tell the numbers. Be brief.

BLACK: Bookseller says twelve sold yesterday,
    Twenty-nine this week, sixty gone this month
    The second edition remains prominently displayed, And

HOBBES: Where the sun hits it?

BLACK: Just there. And—

HOBBES: Good man.

BLACK: Three new pamphlets lettered against you.

HOBBES: Three. Chuck them in the fire, with all critics.

BARTENDER: (*Bringing HOBBES coffee.*) Here you are sir compliments of that
    gentleman in the corner.

HOBBES: (*To the room.*) No thank you gentlemen! I'm not having any coffee
    now gentlemen! Many thanks!

WALDORF: To you Hobbsy, hang all the Bishops!

HOBBES: (*To BLACK.*) God keep me from my admirers.

BLACK: It's good for you to be seen here.

WALDORF: Hang 'em high!

HOBBES: (*To the room.*) 'Ah ha ha,' 'Oh yes,'
  (*To BLACK.*) Third cup I turned down.

BLACK: The People love you.

HOBBES: They don't read my books. They only know my face.
  They say I am a coffee house philosopher, but this is a curse.
  And those that do guzzle my words, hurl these worthless threats.

BLACK: The first pamphlet comes from—

HOBBES: Why should I consume this poison they wish to feed me?
  It will arouse an ill-advised choler, I know it.
  My body always feels the first alarm to war,
  But now in Cromwell's new christened peace,
  I may lay aside my sword and let the barking bishops be.
  But tell who wrote it.

BLACK: That most discontented Bishop.

HOBBES: Derry? I can't bear it. Burn the tract.

WALDORF: What's that some nay sayer? Saying what?

HOBBES: It is nothing old son,
  Some hater we'll ignore

BLACK: You must stay abreast of what is said about you Sir.
  The People do read these tracts that slander you.

HOBBES: Who reads them but us?

BLACK: They sell on the strength of your name,
  You underestimate the size of your Cult.

HOBBES: Keep your voice down, *cult*. It is Loyal Following no more.

WALDORF: (*Coming over.*) What's that some new scandal? Give it here.

BLACK: He's reading it! Then me. Then you and yours after we're done.

HOBBES: No we won't crouch over the Bishop each in a turn,
  Read the accursed thing aloud!

BLACK: A pamphlet entitled: 'The Catching of Leviathan, or the Great Whale demonstrating out of Mr. Hobbes his own works that no man who is thoroughly a Hobbist can be a good Christian…'

HOBBES: Bollocks.

BLACK: '…or a Good Commonwealth man—'

HOBBES: Slanderous Lie

BLACK: 'or reconcile himself to himself—'

HOBBES: To himself to himself to himself…

BLACK: Full stop. 'Because his Principles…'—still the title—'Because his Principles are not only destructive to all Religion but to all Societies… extinguishing the relation between Prince and Subject …'

HOBBES: I spark that relation!

BLACK: '…Parent and Child, Master and Servant…'

WALDORF: Dog and pony.

BLACK: '…Husband and Wife…'

HOBBES: This pamphlet is all title!

BLACK: Semi-colon

HOBBES: Prick.

BLACK: 'And is Inspiration to Atheists all over England.'

Pause.

So signing himself Bishop of Derry,
Proverbs chapter twelve, verse nineteen. What's that?

STATLER: 'The lip of truth shall be established forever…'

HOBBES: 'But a lying tongue is but for a moment.'
This foolish faerie priest wants to sing my swan song from exile?

BLACK: 'Chapter one:'

HOBBES: Oh Bishop of Derry!

If you read me wisely, meaning
Front to back rather than in
Your splattering frenzied way,
You'd know what I write:
All is Material, though it were created by God;
So I don't go in for incantation,
Or transmutation, or any alchemy, I'm truthful and plain.
It is an affront to our distant Creator, whom I believe in,
To claim closeness with Him. Our flesh is far away from God
But I am not an Atheist.

BLACK: Then why stay inside your cave raging, licking wounds,
　　　Letting this exiled cleric attack you,
　　　When he should bow?
　　　Men will only give assent to a strong power,
　　　A crushing power, who throws around great rhetorical weight.
　　　But this Thomas Hobbes would rather retire and hibernate,
　　　And bask in the glow of his most famous book.

HOBBES: Which book is my most famous?

BLACK: Why Leviathan!

A cry of approval!

HOBBES: No cheering!

BLACK: We remember!
　　　Where Hobbes cried against civil war and nonsense,
　　　And now we have stability and no nonsense.
　　　Cromwell. And no King. Hobbes:
　　　The Once and Future Sovereign Power Philosophic in England
　　　Defends His Title!
　　　I like this.
　　　Storms gather in pamphlets unanswered.
　　　Deposed Bishops rise against him,
　　　Then, at once, he strikes back, beats back his nay-sayers—

HOBBES: But I don't fit in your dumb show Black. I feel Fear.
　　　My lovely mother, seven months in, Spanish cannon fire, I pop out,
　　　And Fear was born beside me a twin.
　　　Born into perpetual war an animal, but the man in me wishes for peace.

BLACK: But what of this
    Missive from the exile Edward Hyde
    Suggesting Hobbes betrays his natural king in kneeling before a usurping power.

HOBBES: I never knelt! Whoever keeps Hobbes safe is Sovereign.
    I loved that King, I taught his boy.
    I was the first to flee when factions overwhelmed the crown.
    Does any man remember my exile?

Silence.

    Well fine, it was exile, so is the miserable purpose in exile, to hide.
    In Paris, I daren't make a peep, I ducked all fray and storm with men,
    As best I could I swear it.
    Wrote my book—No cheering—called for a sovereign of any stripe,
    To follow him, whoever, for peace! I'm a peaceful man.
    I returned to my native land not so well assured of safety, but nowhere else was safer;
    It was cold, the snow was deep, I was old,
    The wind was biting and fierce, my horse restive,
    And the road full of pot-holes.
    I returned to this Cromwell Kingdom a wreck, and made amends;
    Cromwell likes Leviathan, hates divine rights: surprise.
    But see the Sovereign etched on the cover was smudged a bit to resemble him, no swindle. Politic is something I see clearly.

BLACK: Why waste your words on the ears in this room?
    This is the pamphlet age of immediate reply and instant attack,
    Come dictate your thoughts to me and claim back the shelves
    These knaves have clogged with their leeching words
    At once!

HOBBES: No my heavy book anchors me here,
    This passing pamphlet river is too shallow for my whaling wisdom,
    It's so narrow I just step right over;
    Plus I'm a man of Peace.
    I am more Magnificent when I use my power not at all
    And disappear my enemies through pointed sharp neglect.

BLACK: But what of this third attack
　　From inside England?
　　A Professor of Mathematics at Oxford.

HOBBES: At Oxford Hobbes is banned.

BLACK: The Bishop John Wallis

HOBBES: These Anglicans are supposed to hide!

BLACK: Saying Hobbes' geometry is 'in sum, all error and railing.'

HOBBES: My Geometry in error?

BLACK: 'Did this man Hobs writ waking or dreaming?' Wallis writes.

HOBBES: I wrote whilst waking, though in dreaming would still outdo him.
　　See this new breed of double deception. Bishop and experimenter in one.

BLACK: Charges of Atheism you can ignore, they are so foolish untrue,
　　But slander against your mathematic foundation begs a killing blow.

HOBBES: The cause of Civil War was factions wanting freedom.
　　This new experimental sect wants freedom from the tested ways,
　　From ways forged in Experience, they want freedom to Experiment.
　　Those Who Would Tell Me What I Do Not See is There,
　　Or what I know I know is out-of-date, fie on them!
　　My ideas don't float on Aire, they walk on land.
　　Oxford stiffs,
　　They lure students as tinkering magicians do, with illusions and swift patter.
　　Publicize themselves mine enemy?
　　I suppose every hiding Anglican from Paris down to Gresham College
　　Where I hear they linger
　　Wants to kidnap my Philosophy and trick it into some perverse disguise,
　　Steal my work and autograph abstracts on top, they are vandals.
　　Calling Hobbes' Geometry Nonsense?
　　I took dictation for Francis Bacon when I was twenty-one and blond,
　　These young molesters crouch behind Frank's statue, cribbing off Hobbes.
　　I'll turn them out. Burn out hiders, silence them for peace.

BLACK: There is no stopping you. No censor would hold you back.
　　Walk hard, conjure your hate, count your enemies' obvious flaws, you always
　　see, then straight after to me dictate your harming thoughts.

HOBBES: Give me Wallis' brief and I will make brief work of it.
　　I will sweat out my response climbing Tower hill,
　　Meet me at my attic Black,
　　In the time it takes you to fetch ink and paper,
　　My words will want your hand. (*Exits.*)

BLACK: Too much paper in the streets catch fire.
　　Likewise with words when the right eyes read them. (*Exits.*)

STATLER: What was that then? He didn't even really begin to answer his nay-Sayers.

WALDORF: You heard him! Something about Paris! (*Regarding pamphlet.*)
　　Look at these shabby things, I could print these ten times better at my shop.

STATLER: You tell me: does that man love Cromwell or hate him?

WALDORF: He loves the sovereign, whoever's sovereign,
　　That's who he loves.

STATLER: Protect his own hide sounds like.

WALDORF: That's government innit?
　　Assent to whatever sovereign thing.

STATLER: Moments like this I miss the King.

　　Exeunt.

1.5

A droning sermon is heard. CHARLES II, seated at Presbyterian table in Scotland, listens to the lengthy grace by PREACHER DOUGLAS.

CHARLES: (*Aside.*) Scottish Presbyterians bore me stiff.
　　Every thing gets a prayer and endless!
　　Does God listen if every peasant and
　　Pauper makes of his supper table a pulpit,
　　To rehearse extra-long sermons'n'prayers
　　And never for a moment stop praising Him
　　On on and on, His divine attention
　　Surrendered completely to the detail and
　　Abundance of dim poor people's prayers?

For shame I don't hear them, they mean well, but *please*.
God must be a consciousness Vast,
Beyond us, unconcerned with the ebb and flow of sin;
Which has much meaning to us, on earth, fine,
But not to God, who wants One for All,
To keep the kingdom on Earth in order.
As to the details, does God care? No No.

PREACHER DOUGLAS: It follows that, when any Certain king getteth the Crown,
He should think it, at Best, a fading Crown...

CHARLES: (*Aside.*) These dirty Scots will raise an army for me
Against Cromwell, if only I promise their Prayer Book to law. Pray whatever.
I will promise any silly thing to make my way back home.

DOUGLAS: Crown worn away by Ages of Transgression,
Crown worn away by Ages of crypto-Popery.

CHARLES: (*Aside.*) This is his subtle message of reproach, meant for me.

DOUGLAS: Crown worn away at the Edges, by Foppery.
Crown worn when men forget Thanksgivings.
Crown worn down to the bone through the marrow, Lord!

CHARLES: (*Aside.*) Now this is only a grace before the meal,
There will be much morbid thanksgiving again at supper's end.
Exile is hell. Look at the filthy fellowship forced upon me, I hate it.
But I live in hope, that soon upon their brutish backs I shall charge back,
And if the People will it, claim my crown.

1.6

A crowded coffeehouse. An auction of books takes place. HOOKE and others are bidding. WILLIS and WILKINS wait to meet ROBERT BOYLE.

WILLIS: This is outrageous. Have I ever been derelict in my Dues?
I paid Dues when it was but my Dues and your Dues made any Dues at all
for this *group*: Our soul booty—and I never missed a payment!
Now my best mechanic traded away under my nose, to curry favor!

WILKINS: We are in Fellowship with Boyle now, Thom.

WILLIS: I never met the man.
Flowy notes, favors from afar, lending coin to our Cause,
Now stealing tools straight from my hands? What next?

AUCTIONEER: Sold to dis gentleman down front, noble lord, thank you kindly.
Next on the block book of math and graphs to tickle the noggin. Start the
bidding kindly at five penny do I have five penny five?

WALLIS: Five pennies.

HOOKE: (*Calling to WILLIS.*) Thom do you have a penny to spare?

WILLIS: (*To HOOKE.*) No!
(*To WILKINS.*) Precious boy, given away to an amateur alchemist with a deep
purse. I thought we were pressing the alchemists out John,
Remember our stealth agenda?

WILKINS: Boyle is not an alchemist. He advocates our same system,
and is keen to build machines with money far beyond our means.

WILLIS: So he spends to steal our thunder
Does he also aim to command our brotherhood?

AUCTIONEER: I have ten pennies then, may I have twelve?
Mouth melting maths and graphs at ten pennies.

STATLER: You know my own boy was lost fighting for the King.

COX: I do uncle.

STATLER: So I have some spare coin to buy you the book you want.

COX: It is coming up. Kind uncle, I will repay you
Just as soon as my glass-working turns a profit.

ROTTEN enters followed by ROBERT BOYLE.

WILKINS: (*Aside.*) Look, Boyle's attendant is there,
And another man, slightly built, that is Boyle,
Coming for the boy,

BOYLE: (*Aside to ROTTEN.*) I can scarcely think, the din is so tremendous

WILKINS: (*Aside to WILLIS.*) Thom, I beg you, make no trouble. Wear a false
smile and trust me, you must; this is the surest course for our group.

ROTTEN: (*Aside.*) There is John Wilkins, he is a fawner prepare yourself.

WILLIS: (*Aside.*) God forgive this false smile on my face

BOYLE: (*Aside.*) Oh how I detest this ritual of patronage,
Their flattery is like to make me very queasy

ROTTEN: John Wilkins, Thomas Willis, may I present the honorable Robert Boyle.

WILKINS: The honorable Robert Boyle, Virtuoso, welcome.

BOYLE: Brother Wilkins, God bless.
I can scarcely conceal the joy I feel meeting you,
Seeing you bring together brothers from all over England.
Your Invisible Group is flourishing.

WILKINS: By your patronage.

BOYLE: Now I join you, and we can mission our great work beyond these shuttered rooms.

WILKINS: There was never a jot of doubt in my heart that we were brothers, Robert. Sharing a common Christian wish for Progress in all quarters, and peace. You are welcome here among us, and your servant.

WALLIS: Virtuoso, I am John Wallis. My work is in Geometry.

ROTTEN: Wallis, Wilkins, Willis. W, w, w: easy to recall.

BOYLE: Do you still observe the stars Brother Wilkins?

WILKINS: Lately I have observed the Moon,
And thought should it not be a colony for England?
Imagine the peace on her surface!

WALLIS: I have drawn a sign for infinity,
They said infinity was impossible to draw, but I drew it.

BOYLE: I have heard tale of you, Dr. Willis, Your mighty reckoning with the guts of creation,
Anatomy I think, is marvelous.

WILLIS: I wonder will those gentle hands of yours be reckoning with the guts, Virtuoso?

BOYLE: I study not the bloody things,
    And do gather hands not so gentle as my own, to build.
    But then my eyes are never clouded by pride in the instruments,
    Which can make a man like to ignore errors,
    Or smudge the facts for vanity at his own handicraft.
    This way I witness plain.

WILKINS: Dove-ish words, quite divine.

BOYLE: And so…

WILKINS: Yes, yonder is the young man whom I recommend to you.
    Thomas, tell him about the boy.

WILLIS: Robert Hooke:
    Wandered over from the Isle White, found his way to London,
    Friendless thirteen year old with ten pound in his pocket.
    I caught him drawing circles around some poor painter,
    Titled apprentice whilst he embarrassed the master.
    Took him on. Quite a find.
    Of course, if upon trial, or error,
    You are dissatisfied with the boy,
    I'll have him back.

WILKINS: Not that we prefer him, only that we mean to serve you properly

WILLIS: What I meant.

BOYLE: Is the boy a member of our suppressed Church?

WILKINS: He attends our private worship regularly.

BOYLE: Does he harbor any dogma or superstition from his country life.

WILLIS: He harbors a stubborn secrecy, when it comes to his designs.

BOYLE: Has he been told of his new employment?

WILKINS: Did you tell him?

WILLIS: I only just learned—

WILKINS: Tell the boy tell the boy.

BOYLE: I shall introduce myself.

ROTTEN: Come gentlemen, does this auction house serve beer?

WILLIS: I'll have beer, but you're buying.

AUCTIONEER: Now I don't speak any French gentlemen
So you'll pardon my French on these ones here:
'*Revolvus Orbitus Solestium*' Copernicus,
Sounds racy! No pictures! We will start the bidding at one shilling.

STATLER: One.

MAN 1: Two shillings.

HOOKE: Too rich!

BOYLE: Is that the book you want?

HOOKE: That isn't the one.

STATLER: Three.

MAN 1: Four.

BOYLE: Four is a good price. Pity I own it already.

HOOKE: Lucky man.

STATLER: Five.

BOYLE: So I see you are bit crooked. Is this why you are called Hooke?

MAN 1: Six shillings.

HOOKE: My name is Robert Hooke, baptized that way,

STATLER: Seven.

HOOKE: The crooked back came later, a cruel joke.

MAN 1: Eight.

HOOKE: To echo the name. So the name echoes.

STATLER: Nine.

HOOKE: But do you know me, sir?

AUCTIONEER: I have a bid of nine shillings gentlemen.

BOYLE: I require assistance in the manufacture of some experimental apparatus.

AUCTIONEER: All done?

HOOKE: Then you must talk to Doctor Willis…

AUCTIONEER: All done?

HOOKE: I work for him.

AUCTIONEER: Nine going once.

BOYLE: I have spoken to Doctor Willis, and the secretary Wilkins.

AUCTIONEER: Going twice.

BOYLE: Now you work for me.

AUCTIONEER: Sold to you Neddy good run.

BOYLE: I will assume your expense and command your hands,
    At my own laboratory. My name is Robert Boyle.

HOOKE: Oh.

AUCTIONEER: Next on the block: 'Socrates Philosophia'
    Not much wear and tear. One shilling.

BOYLE: Your demonstrations are fine science.
    I confess I snatched a glance at some distance:
    To watch you open that dog for Doctor Willis.
    Your command of the witnessing crowd is wonderful,

AUCTIONEER: May I have one shilling? Greek Philosophia, oo la la.

HOOKE: But then you know me from error.
    That bit with the dog was a soggy shambles, my instrument failed.

BOYLE: I do greatly pity the dog.

HOOKE: It is unfashionable to pity the dog but I do.

BOYLE: Me too.

AUCTIONEER: One shilling? Nobody?

BOYLE: But error is part of Progress, if your course is true.

The miracle in experiment is Instant Witness, truth unadorned.
A democracy of seeing is my aim. With this Peace can be achieved,
And with God's blessing dispute: extinguished.
I will help you wipe away the blood, and experiment in more exalted ways.

HOOKE: Then, Robert Boyle, if this is true,
And you assume my expense,
I will be a keen mechanic and builder for you,
And by my unflinching industry your patronage shall be requited
In full.

WALDORF: Boy who bought you that book?

COX: My own coin father, from the work I've done.

AUCTIONEER: Next item I'm told is rare: '*La description du corps humain.*'
Another deliciously French book, bursting with illustration.

HOOKE: Pardon sir this is the one I want.

AUCTIONEER: We'll start the bidding at six pence. Six pence?

HOOKE: Six!

AUCTIONEER: Six pence to the ugly boy in the back!

HOOKE: Thank God he started low.

MAN 2: Eight pence.

HOOKE: Nine pence!

MAN 2: Two shillings.

HOOKE: Drat.

MAN 1: Three shillings.

HOOKE: Um three shillings tuppence?

MAN 2: Four.

HOOKE: Oh Miserable coins! That is Descartes in French, I've lost it.

MAN 1: Six shillings.

MAN 2: Eight shillings.

AUCTIONEER: I have eight! May I have nine shillings gentlemen?

BOYLE: Nine shillings.

AUCTIONEER: Nine from the Bishop there, gentlemen.

BOYLE: (*To HOOKE.*) I am not a Bishop.

AUCTIONEER: May I have ten?

HOOKE: Thank you Sir, here have my three.

BOYLE: Keep your three, the book's for me.

AUCTIONEER: Are we all done at nine shillings?

BOYLE: You will explain Descartes' ideas to me.

HOOKE: I had but three shillings to spend.

BOYLE: On the book?

HOOKE: This month.

AUCTIONEER: All done?

WILLIS stumbles over, drunk.

WILLIS: What is the commotion?

AUCTIONEER: Nine shillings going once?

BOYLE: I am buying a book young Robert lusted after.

AUCTIONEER: Nine going twice?

WILLIS: Buying? I thought this was an auction?

BOYLE: It is an auction.

WILLIS: Then I bid ten.

AUCTIONEER: Ten shillings! A Miracle! French Books Prove Popular Today!

BOYLE: Dr. Willis, what are you doing?

WILLIS: I want that one.

BOYLE: I am buying it.

AUCTIONEER: May I have twelve from the Bishop?

WILLIS: Well, I'm sorry Robert but I placed my bid.

BOYLE: Twelve! I am buying the book for Robert here.

WILLIS: Fourteen shillings! (*Digging in his pockets.*)

HOOKE: Do you have that Thom?

BOYLE: Do not raise the price for the sake of raising it.

WILLIS: Fourteen isn't much to pay.

BOYLE: You will force me to propose a sum quite beyond your grasp Dr. Willis.

AUCTIONEER: Fourteen going once.

WILLIS: I should like to marvel at such a conspicuous sum.

AUCTIONER: Twice gentlemen.

BOYLE: One pound sterling.

AUCTIONEER: A rock! Sterling! Gentlemen. Going once!

BOYLE: (*To AUCTIONEER.*) Bring me the book.

The book is passed to BOYLE.

WILLIS: I only think, in the future, one might inform me as to any potential change in servants, so providing me good time to find replacement, though, unhappily, and in this special case, none exists. Oh thank you!

ROTTEN: This man drank my whole purse, I need another.

WILLIS: Let history remember, I employed him first.

BOYLE: (*To HOOKE:*) Now to my laboratory. I have all these books Robert. And one more. For you.

BOYLE, HOOKE and ROTTEN exit. BLACK enters.

BLACK: (*To the room.*) I have a message and a gift for the geometric John Wallis!

WALLIS: I am he.

BLACK approaches WALLIS.

BLACK: I deliver to you a reasoned reply by one Thomas Hobbes, the great
philosopher, refuting your late hateful tract—and this message from him:
'Be warned! Spies and Snakes are not favored in this new age, and would be
well-advised to slide back under rocks and leave great men alone.'

WALLIS: Am I a spy? Go away knave. Your master's a liar. He will say anything
to distract his faction from the horrible errors in his gross geometry.
Claiming to Square the Circle? Be gone filthy messenger

1.7

*ROBERT BOYLE's laboratory. HOOKE is sitting alone with his belongings. ROTTEN
enters.*

ROTTEN: You stand in this room until he rises.
You should be standing when he comes in.

HOOKE: How long until he wakes?

ROTTEN: He takes physic, and replenishes with naps.
Not so long to wait, I tidy the work table, run one errand to the chemist, by
then he rises. So the tidying imagine a usual tidying, and one to the chemists,
a few thousand steps.

HOOKE is wearing a watch on his wrist tied with a ribbon.

Oh you have a clock. I can't tell you in Minnitts.

Pause.

How many Minnitts does it say you have been waiting?

HOOKE: (*Staring.*) It has been, it says, nearly thirty minutes.

ROTTEN: How can that be so?

HOOKE: My own design.
It is driven by the vibrations of a special spring,
An improvement on The Pendulum.

ROTTEN: Yes yes I know The Pendulum. I'm not so foolish.

HOOKE: Bit difficult to put together that. I venture no man in London makes one better. Have a look. Wrist Watch. Accurate to within two or three hours on a given day.

ROTTEN: Two or three. Most impressive.

Pause.

HOOKE: Are you a servant?

ROTTEN: I am an actor.

Pause.

An actor.
Oh you've not seen a show ever I suppose.

HOOKE: I never left this country my life.

ROTTEN: Am I so old? I played on English stages, one time ago. You don't remember. Mostly the parts of women. I was beautiful, twisted babe. You could like a play.

HOOKE: What's it like?

ROTTEN: I pray God's forgiveness when I think of what
May come to the sons and daughters of this isle
If they are forever deprived of Art.
They'll all be lost in watches, they'll forget about
The tendons, forget the veiny way of life.

Pause.

You perform well.

HOOKE: Pardon me?

ROTTEN: A performer.

HOOKE: No.

ROTTEN: No why?

HOOKE: The appeal is to Reason, I hope. Is that performing?

ROTTEN: Ambitious boy: It is.

BOYLE enters.

ROTTEN: Virtuoso, you're awake.

BOYLE: And dreamt deep. But, Daniel Rotten, loyal man,
    I must discuss the substance of my great work with our boy, here.
    Go, and close the door behind you.

ROTTEN: What is the substance a secret my Grace?

BOYLE: It would only bore you: the details; take leave.

ROTTEN: Boring stood outside the door you know.

BOYLE: Go wander then; close the door behind you.

ROTTEN: It is nearly five isn't it?

HOOKE: It's half three.

BOYLE: Take leave.

ROTTEN exits.

Enough noise: those stories out there, go quiet, in here.
Here is my mind's sacred space for thinking,
And your hands equipped to build;
The substance of our great work is to discover Facts absent any Passion,
Truth witnessed plain. Facts with no guesses attached.
We employ no absurd words here, no words at all if I'm happy.
Our findings will never reflect ourselves, they will only point back to our
Creator.

HOOKE: What of Knowledge will we rely on?

BOYLE: None, for Knowledge is an old, handed-down thing.
    Knowledge is earth-bound,
    It is too near to a fireside story corrupted by man,
    Facts are fresh and pure, they are innocent of man's intent,
    They are universal things, incorruptible; and if a fact is over-turned, it
    vanishes,
    It never was a fact. I've noticed knowledge hangs around, it hangs on men.
    We will be more than men, we will be Divines.
    It takes patience to proceed this way.

HOOKE: I am diligent.

BOYLE: Do you know Humility? Is your eye faithful?

HOOKE: My eye is faithful.

BOYLE: Is your hand true? Can you motion Aire with precision?
    What do you know of Aire?

HOOKE: I confess to know little about it.

BOYLE: And so I know less. But there we start.
    See, Hooke, the work of this German;
    He makes a copper barrel, in two halves,
    And a kind of pump, to remove Aire from the barrel,
    And this Guericke writes that a dozen horses could not pull the halves apart,
    So great was the strength when Aire is sucked out.
    But in this German's copper barrel, no one witnesses the Aire in it's rare condition.
    His vessel tests the strength of horses,
    Ours should be built for witnessing.

HOOKE: In a barrel?

BOYLE: But not in a barrel; Glass globe chamber, large enough to see.
    And some mechanical measure, to remove the Aire: A pump;
    Think how it might fit tight and be secure of Aire, to your devising,
    Think on the mechanics, and what tools, whilst to the Glassman:
    Christopher Cox;
    There order the largest globe he makes, bargain hard,
    Watch him blow and shape the globe,
    Devise your pump, somehow, to remove the Aire,
    Motion it to and fro, make it dense, or thin within the chamber.
    Inside this globe we will make all manner of experiments,
    And Make Aire Dance. Think on that.

HOOKE: I am thinking now. Virtuoso, I am home.

BOYLE: My mother tells me when I was a boy,
    Even then possessed by a retreating humor,
    A certain gentle stance on earth, then too delicate,
    That my first words to her were 'Shhh',

And in that brief communion she forever after saw my soul.
Our first moments together here burn in my chest,
I feel them now, and will not forget them,
I take this radiant heat to mean you are my spirit's familiar,
Mirror of my soul's inquiry and kindred missioner to the horizon of
Enlightenment,
Where wisdom meets the universe, to reinvent the light.

Pause.

In trial our globes will shatter, tell Cox we are never idle
The first will surely break, the next will crack; get a good price.

HOOKE: I take leave.

TRANSITION. ROTTEN joins STATLER and WALDORF in the street.

ROTTEN: That's me out in the cold then. They're thick as thieves now. Pray,
Tell me Gentlemen, did you ever know fortune to swing so violently to
and fro?

STATLER: Sure fortune swings, that's fortune.

WALDORF: What's so violent about it? Your master has a new favorite.
Happens to every dog in this world.

STATLER: Fortune's violent swing is one of the unique characteristics of this
rotten age we live in.

1.8

A dark, devilish bar in London. HOBBES and BLACK together.

HOBBES: With apologies to all you square pegs, my hole is round.
Shake a tree and cowards fall out, I should know, I numbered among them.
But today I took a stand. I put ale between me and my blind rage,
And set about writing a vicious missive at that knave, Bishop Wallis.
By vicious missive I mean really a reasoned attack.
Ya twisted my arm. Black fellow there, look upon him.

HOBBES raises BLACK's hand.

This devil tempts me thus, to defend my honor,

For plain men God ordains humility, peace,
But great men have Mantles. What of my Mantle? Who will uphold it?

HOBBES goes to piss. ROTTEN enters.

BLACK: Rotten my long lost!

ROTTEN: That's me out in the cold then.

BLACK: Where did you get that coat?

ROTTEN: Pray tell Black, did you ever know fortune to swing so violently to
and fro?

BLACK: Never in all my days.

ROTTEN: Curse that Tyrant Cromwell, curse him!
I've lost all sorts of work under him,
Look what I've done to earn meat!
I was born to jest and dance,
Not play the toady behind the scenes and get shit on.
Curse Cromwell and curse that crippleback who has distracted my master.

BLACK: What master?

ROTTEN: A man at Gresham.

BLACK: That's the place my man attacks. Full of snakes.
You can help us smoke them out.

ROTTEN: I might have been an esteemed society Gentlemen
But now I'm cast out no doubt for the lowness of my blood.
It shows through.

BLACK: On you? Not at all.

ROTTEN: The make-up won't wash off.

BLACK: You are Adonis if not Venus in my eyes.
Look at our huge hands. We are Gods!

ROTTEN: Large beer!

BLACK: Rotten, gorgeous man, drinks on me, for I have gold today,
I found a game for us—I even tread a board today and spoke,

Though my audience was uninvited and my interlocutor utterly shocked. I commanded a crowd, for a moment, and embarrassed one Gresham geometric.

ROTTEN: Doing what?

BLACK: It begins with written attacks, dictated to me by this man of controversy Thomas Hobbes.

ROTTEN: (*Disgusted.*) Scribing? More beer.

BLACK: Rotten, our old craft is crushed. Men want a bloody battle of ideas.

HOBBES: (*Returning.*) How many pints is that boys?

BLACK: Six father, and you?

HOBBES: I'm finishing my second pint, and here's me, twice as drunk as the both of you. Proving, again, my Principle of Wheat.

BLACK: What Principle father?

HOBBES: The intoxicant will outlast the wheat, so take small sips, drink slowly, the sugar dissipates naturally, and you'll be pissed twice as long. These stiffs behind the bar don't want me saying it.

ROTTEN: The man is near ninety and wants us to marvel it only takes him one pint to piss.

HOBBES: Young people forget how to drink. Might no hereditary wisdom pass between generations in this age of perpetual unrest?

ROTTEN: We possess the stamina of youth. Me and Black here, we're in our Prime. It takes gallons of drink to fell us. You're counting backwards in pints Mate.

HOBBES: Who is this?

BLACK: Mr. Rotten. An actor.

HOBBES: Actor? Poor fox.

ROTTEN: You saw my Volpone?

HOBBES: Whatever tripe. I wouldn't boast yourself an actor my boy, it makes men uncomfortable, your silly dreams. We, good people, wish to be protected

and shielded from that perfect storm of desperation which hangs like stink
on any fairy wants to tread the boards a lady.

ROTTEN: I was treated better at Gresham.

HOBBES: Enemy in our midst!

BLACK: Not an enemy, an asset in our fight.
    Rotten was fired by a Gresham Divine,
    And has seen their experiments up close.

HOBBES: But has he been enchanted?
    Mr Rotten, I hate to tell you: These new priests of Nature,
    You so foolishly served, want to wind us up,
    Ditch my system, start over fresh and say:
    'Ah we know nothing until we stare at rocks.'
    They want to investigate existence in order,
    Starting from scratch, mice first, no smaller: dust first,
    They stare at that for years, dust…
    Then onto the properties of jam; Insanity: Experiments!
    A real philosopher instantly Knows, he doesn't go poking,
    Experience is King.

ROTTEN: (*Aside to BLACK.*) You want me to play vassal to this old blowhard?

BLACK: (*Aside to ROTTEN.*) You will help me devise an even sharper way to slay
his foes.

HOBBES: A toast to our experiment! This, for them, is an experiment!
    Can you comprehend that? We drink some pints,
    Notice the variety in how men get pissed, and establish a Principle.
    But they are scientists,
    So they get lobsters pissed and trust that principle instead.
    Or set six pints and a half dozen eel, dissect the corpses and marvel at that,
    In the end they discover: Wheat Metabolizes as Sugar in the Blood!
    Read Hobbes, save time, save lobsters.
    They miss a chance to get pissed and call it the New Philosophy!

1.9

ROBERT BOYLE's laboratory. HOOKE, WILLIS and COX stand about the Pneumatic Engine.

HOOKE: At first I sealed the lip with lard,
Then we learned that salad oil works best to seal it.
There are some leaks still, which you hear whistling
When we condense the Aire.
The globes will often shatter.
I shattered so many of these in trial, this one is new.

WILLIS: What does it do?

HOOKE: Thank you Christopher.

COX: May I stay and watch it work?

HOOKE: No Chris go.

COX exits.

He musn't see how it all fits together.
Thom, this chamber will be utterly void of Aire.
There will be no Aire in there.
In this one place on earth, there will be nothing at all.

WILLIS: Does it have to do with breathing?

HOOKE: It has to do with Nothing. It is Matter isolated from Aire, I'll show you.
We don't have any baby chicks to snuff. I'll do the one with coal.

HOOKE places a lump of glowing coal in the Pneumatic Engine chamber.

WILLIS: How can you remove all the Aire?

HOOKE: With these twisted black greasy hands I pump,
Several vigorous minutes, and labor against the leaks,
It fills again quickly if I don't maintain it,
That is my job whilst Boyle does the sermon.

WILLIS: How much did he pay to have this built?

HOOKE: Thousands of pounds, you wouldn't believe it if you saw the bills
And Boyle pays without winking. Working inside his pockets is roomy,

Thom I'm a convert, Progress is in the funding.

WILLIS: Irish plantations buy England great tools.
The Honorable Robert Boyle's Noble Pneumatic Engine.
Sounds like a poem.
And here, some boy that helped him out.

HOOKE: He depends on my design. I'm due to be a big man in Science Thom.

HOOKE begins to work the brass pump and vacate the chamber of air.

WILLIS: Properties of Aire in the abstract is a nice pursuit for an honored Earl,
but invisible substance is difficult to sell. When I discover the connection
between breathing and Aire, people will care.

HOOKE: The grandest and the smallest revelations should be seen side by side.

WILLIS: Boyle has made it plain he doesn't respect medical practice.
Because I make my own money treating patients he mistrusts me.
Your new master is blessed he can so afford to pursue these esoteric
questions.

HOOKE: Now when the chamber is almost empty, I signal Boyle to begin,
He strides to a place three meters from the pump and speaks:
'When a man is lawful master onto his senses; keen, patient, and true…'
Blah blah.
Just as Boyle ends, the Aire is nearly gone, my leaks are hissing,
And you see the ember's glow diminish with each successive round of
pumping.
I slow my arm. See there:
The spring in Aire is tightened, and the glow goes slack,
Aire has spring.
And we see that fire needs Aire to be fire.
Fire is not an element. Fire 'as seen here plainly' is a chemical reaction
Of some kind.

WILLIS: Of what kind?

HOOKE: Boyle says it is hubris to guess. I have twenty-seven of my own
conjecture, I tuck away for deeper looking. But here we only demonstrate out
how Nature has laws, that it never deviates; a steady hand made this world:
The Great Architect.

WILLIS: It is a nice little miracle Robert.

HOOKE: Don't look at me that way.

WILLIS: How am I looking at you?

ROBERT BOYLE enters.

BOYLE: Throw a sheet over the pump,
The others will be here soon. Let us reveal it to them shall we?
But here you are preparing, in your spare time, diligent mechanic.

HOOKE: Sir you remember Thom Willis.

BOYLE: Of course Thom, you are welcome here, this is a safe place to pray.

WILLIS: It is shameful that we must hide our Anglican church ways behind trap
windows and lab doors.

WILKINS and WALLIS enter.

WILKINS: Virtuoso your laboratory is grand.

BOYLE: Welcome all, Gentlemen, the Pneumatic Engine, let me unveil it.

WALLIS: (*Holds up a pamphlet.*) I want to know whose eyes are polluted by
this trash.

WILKINS: Apologies your honor,
John has had his heart enflamed by another pamphlet written against him.

WALLIS: Does this circulate in the street? Boy what do you know of Thomas
Hobbes?

BOYLE: We can discuss those quarrels later.

HOOKE: He is some aged thinker from inside England, nearer now to Socrates
age than my own.

WALLIS: Does this poison course in coffee houses or is it obscure?

HOOKE: It courses.

WALLIS: This dog Hobbes, who has taken officious care excusing our current
Tyrant.

WILKINS: Soften yourself John.

WILLIS: Can we not hate Cromwell in private?

WALLIS: Listen: 'Six Lessons to Bishop Wallis, Professor of Mathematics…'
Then he spends ages excusing himself, evoking Vespasian's Law, God knows
what, saying his vitriol is revenge for the rules of propriety broken by me in
previous tracts.

BOYLE: How many tracts have you sent against him?

WALLIS: But three. Debunking his geometry. Nothing to prompt this,
Every word I wrote was truthful and scholarly, can he say the same?

BOYLE: Then add your proofs to our book of Facts and leave dispute aside John.

WILKINS: Hobbes' hate touches all of us here.

WALLIS: 'You Uncivil Ecclessiastics,' he writes, 'Inhuman Divines,
De-doctors of Morality, Egregious Isaachers.

WILLIS: Isaachers?

WALLIS: I said it is vitriolic!

WILKINS: A dogmatic never revises his views.

WALLIS: 'You do know how to trouble and subvert strong Government'

WILKINS: This when we have done all to appease and conform.

WALLIS: 'Divinity may go on in Gresham, but only to furnish the pulpit with
men to cry down the Civil Power.'

WILLIS: This Hobbes is so fast to hide behind Cromwell's shield, though he
tutored our true and natural King in boyhood, his coward's heart comes
through.

WALLIS: 'They may appear to submit loyally, but it is known their Romanized
Church ways are still practiced in secret.'

Pause.

'And as for that nice doctor Wallis,' here about me:
'His Geometry is Experimenting Jargon
He is among those monied Bishops at Gresham claiming to weigh Aire.'
This man hates us. And I hate him the more.

HOOKE: What is his true objection to our work Virtuoso?

WILKINS: He rages against phantom teachers from his youth sixty years ago.

WILLIS: It is a ploy to sell more books, and touch our growing fame with his critique.

WALLIS: He doesn't understand a single lick of geometry!

BOYLE: This Hobbes sees monsters.
    A philosopher like that trusts his fleshy sense and wit alone,
    And wants us to leave unknowns unknown.
    He fears mystery and misreads Nature, because boy,
    The man does not believe in God.

LORD BROGHILL enters.

BOYLE: Brother.

BROGHILL: Sweet brother.

WILKINS: Lord Broghill.

BROGHILL: Gentlemen, I have only halted here a moment, to speak with my brother, aside.

BOYLE and BROGHILL stand aside.

BOYLE: Where have you been?

BROGHILL: Cromwell is dead. Dead in his bed, from illness,
    And his son has quickly tumbled down. The Rump is recalled.
    The purged return.
    I fear the Rump tips with men loyal to a certain King,
    Charles' son is like to return and rule.
    Our Republic shakes.
    I will go West, to command father's land in Munster.
    Our family, brother, will offer that land for bounty to the new sovereign,
    And with this gift make amends for my part in Cromwell's rule,
    Which is like to be exhumed in a new kingdom, I shall shoulder that,
    And lay low on father's land. (*To all:*)
    Cromwell is dead.
    You spotless church loyals, virtuosi, I advise you: stay in London,
    Flood in, fill the gaps,

Dampen the fiery rage in this city, in men,
Which threatens to unseat the Civil Power.
I will return when our family's position is secure.

BOYLE: I pity your journey brother, but promise with all my heart,
To publish peace in every gesture, every action of mine,
Our New Science will heal sick hearts in England, brother, away,
My own heart is sick to see you flee like this.

BROGHILL: I return to our father's land, so envy me,
It is Eden in May, if I make it. (*Exits.*)

1.10

A stormy day in London. WALDORF comes upon HOBBES.

WALDORF: Sir, you'll not believe it,
A shriek of fire, lighting from that cloud yonder
Struck a horse dead at Blackfriars, one unholy shot:
Dead. All the men standing about: 'A sign!
A sign!' Like apes. 'A sign! Tell our fate Lord!'
I only know the horses' fate, four legs straight up in the air.

HOBBES: Why are men such fools?
I will calm them, explain away the devil, it is no sign of doom,
Only an excess cold wind, forced out by the motion of the clouds.

TRANSITION. At the body of a dead horse struck by lightning.

HOOKE is crouched over the body with COX, STATLER and the DRIVER.

HOOKE: It is as if a bolt, or small cannon ball shot straight down.

COX: I smelt brimstone Robert, when I turned to look,
The horse was dead, her driver thrown back ten steps and singed.
Had I been standing out here…God he knows.
I have your latest globe Robert, inside.

DRIVER: She took the lightning for me, poor girl.

HOOKE: Sulfur in the air, but where are the burns?

STATLER: It is a sign gentlemen. A Providential sign the King will come.

WALDORF: Or that he won't.

DRIVER: It's a sign that I am cursed. Now, without a horse.

HOOKE: Cox, go inside your shop, bring out your eye-glass,
　　We can observe the flesh closely to see if lightning leaves any trace.
　　If it is a flame, where is the combustion?
　　Do you smell sulfur now? I smell nothing.

　　HOBBES arrives with WALDORF. ROTTEN and BLACK arrive aside.

HOBBES: What here? Are tinkers and bottle-blowers pondering providence?
　　Spotting signs in the violent motion of weather?
　　All this is easily explained, Gentlemen.
　　Put away your working tools, bind up your wounds driver,
　　I will use my mind to put you all at ease.

WALDORF: Listen to this man Christopher, his sense is pure.

HOOKE: (*To COX.*) Why does this fool run down our tools?

HOBBES: The cause of all things is Motion.
　　It is not fire, lightning, rather a sudden cold wind,
　　That freezes what it strikes.
　　Clear away this horse.

HOOKE: Keep it here.
　　Has your law seen up close horse flesh seared by lightning?
　　Underneath a microscope? The Senses can be expanded.

ROTTEN: (*To BLACK.*) That is the usurping worm.

BLACK: (*Calling to HOBBES.*) Disciples of the New Science!

HOBBES: Ah! They practice the newest superstition, Experimenta.
　　Yes with baited breath we wait to hear what you will add to my physics.
　　It will be a marvelous footnote no doubt, full of detail. Keep in touch.
　　They will only find some evidence proves me true, down there, kneeling with
　　fancy glass, saying words and speaking tongues,
　　But thank God I possess a prudent mind, gracefully aged,
　　And so I know what is knowable already.
　　Not by rote, or weird invention, but by my own true faculty of Reason.

COX: What are we meant to accept that but by the bare affirmation of your
    words?

HOBBES: My words are for men of sense,
    Not for baby-birds with mouths upturned to preacher's puke.

BLACK: (*To ROTTEN.*) See the crowd gather. They will belong to us soon.

HOOKE: Meaner minds begin at the beginning, kneeling here if need be.

HOBBES: He says 'meaner minds' as if he has an army behind him.
    Tell boy, who are you?

HOOKE: I am assistant to England's finest Natural Philosopher.

HOBBES: Bite your tongue. I know thee not.

HOOKE: Nor I you, and what of it? My employer is Robert Boyle.

HOBBES: But the finest Philosopher in England is Thomas Hobbes,
    So you have been misled.

HOOKE: A man saluting Hobbes could only be Hobbes himself.

HOBBES: He has heard of me. You are redeemed.

HOOKE: I have heard of him. I've heard of Hobbes.
    On Motion, he gets it wrong,
    He adds nothing to Francis Bacon,
    On Politics I have no comment,
    And his Geometry, as I hear it, is laughably false.
    His law from the top refuses new facts from the bottom:
    Hobbes the false Idol!
    We kneel before Nature to see it,
    That is Creation, men meant to stoop!
    Bodies may appear to change when mechanics look close,
    But facts won't mold themselves into any old fool system,
    That I can swear to.

WALDORF: Little radical needs two more lumps on his head.

STATLER: (*To WALDORF.*) Attend the argument and learn.

HOBBES: You are my student,
    Your mouth makes sounds that come from me.

Long before clever boys read books, I wrote them.
I write the books men read; you recite because you don't know better.
I spit on kids that challenge me.
Hobbes already preached down against dogma in thought,
This is our crisis in England,
In this changing, leaderless time, many diseased ideas will grow.
Every man and boy now wants to follow his own faith,
But my humble scribble still stands as an honest account of the all the knowledge I know. You live in darkness.
Step into my light you might go blind.
Never step into my light Goddamnit it, never. You don't want it.
You might shit your pants, stepping in my light.
Refuse my doctrine at your peril parlous boy.

HOOKE: Forgive us, the new minds in London
Trust our own hands and eyes to reveal God's Creation.
I won't be a philosopher if that word means
Some wordy duffer whose practice is but a Fancy Brain Activity,
Swearing on uncertain horse-shit with a rounded oath.
Dad we do refuse it.

HOBBES: Does the boy mock me when he calls me 'Dad'?
But when we have at it, I'll make you my Son,
Sun you, so bright, my shadow will fall heavy across your scoffing face.

ROBERT BOYLE enters.

BOYLE: Robert, come back to lab. Rainy hours are the best for working.

HOOKE: I am coming Master Boyle. Leave this horse to a butcher. (*To COX.*) Get me our globe.

HOBBES: (*Calling after BOYLE.*) Honorable Earl, your name's in the street.

BLACK: (*To ROTTEN.*) This battle will launch ten more pamphlets, all the better for us.

Exeunt.

1.11

Many men waiting for CHARLES II to pass on his way to the Coronation.

STATLER: It is a vacuum.

WALDORF: A what?

STATLER: They built a vacuum.

WALDORF: A vacuum what?

STATLER: A zone of nothing.

WALDOLF: You're telling me to believe in nothing? I thought your squad claimed to be Christians. Now they worship a spirit called Vacuum?

STATLER: It's not a spirit. You have to see it to believe it.

WALDORF: How do you see nothing? They tell you you can see something when nothing is there? Or is vacuum a new name for something that was always never there?

STATLER: No.

WALDORF: But we got a word for that. The word you used: 'Nothing'. Why do we need another?

STATLER: It's going to piss rain isn't it?

WALDORF: Did I win the argument then?

STATLER: We shouldn't be fighting on this historic day.

TRANSITION.

HOBBES: Hope he remembers the good old days,
Me teaching him Latin and the like, his tutor,
And pray he won't notice I lived peacefully
Underneath his enemies iron roof,
As many have done. I am not special.
I could tell him that. The King will listen.

BLACK: What will you say to him?

HOBBES: I do not know. Can you see my hands shaking?

BLACK: I cannot see them shake.

HOBBES: Good, then my inward self is masked,
　　Not without great effort. Inside my very soul I shake,
　　But see I've got a good grip on my hands.

ROTTEN: How quickly do you think, will he pass this spot?
　　Will he stop and we all kneel, or do we kneel even when he passes at a good
　　pace? I should think this one would prefer cheering over kneeling.
　　But I could be wrong.

HOBBES: You won't be kneeling
　　As soon as the King comes you leg it over there.
　　I cannot be seen by the Sovereign to have a faction,
　　I am appearing here as a private citizen expressing simple loyalty.

BLACK: Well so are we.

HOBBES: Not near me. Leg it over there when he comes.

ROTTEN: Will you ask him about the theatres?
　　Ask if he will rebuild them.

HOBBES: Those are rubble. You are stuck with me.
　　You think this King is here to stay? Use your mind man.
　　Amid this naïve parade of hope,
　　And showy bonfires; the grins are strained, the cheers too loud.
　　Hope begins to taste bitter, the more we swallow down.
　　I am an old man, though I don't look it,
　　And all this kneeling is routine to me.
　　See I fall on my right knee today,
　　But save the left for later, should the sovereign change shape,
　　And any one needs new loyalty from me, a new knee.

BLACK: You are too dark, The King loves you,
　　And look around – men do love the King –

WALDORF: Here he comes!

　　TRANSITION

WILKINS: There, look smart, can you stand up any straighter?

HOOKE: This is me standing straight. Aren't we meant to kneel?

WILKINS: Stand behind me, Robert, or stand aloof.
    I agreed you will hand over the gift. But not speak.
    I will speak to the King.

HOOKE: If my design is the gift, I should do the talking.

WILKINS: You are too long in Boyle's lab, you forget yourself,
    You will advance, in due time, and earn freedom,
    But now I do the talking.

HOOKE: Allow me to explain to the king the superiority in my design,
    So he fully appreciates the gift.

WILKINS: Hold your tongue. You would talk down to a King.
    The watch is fine, it speaks for itself, take your flattery from me,
    Stand straight. Here is the King.

STATLER: The king!

A flourish. CHARLES passes. BROGHILL is with him. WILKINS steps forward.

WILKINS: Heaven-sent sovereign, I present to you,
    A Watch, on behalf of—

HOOKE: Which has a special vibrating spring.

WILKINS: I present to you gracious sovereign, a Watch,
    On behalf of fifty-five certain virtuous men at Gresham,
    Who do conduct science experiments in public,
    In the bright new light of your glorious Restoration.

CHARLES: Nice watch. I keep this?

WILKINS: It is a gift from we your fellow explorers in nature,
    We have noted your discoveries through telescopes, which we wish to
    include—

CHARLES: You build telescopes?

HOOKE/WILKINS: Of course your majesty.

HOOKE: Anything you wish.
    We are the finest craftsman and mechanics in your kingdom.

CHARLES: Next!

WILKINS: At your pleasure, loving King.

HOOKE: Enjoy the watch.

CHARLES: Next!

A brief flourish. CHARLES moves on.

Here I spot a shiny grey head,
One I remember. Rise old man.
Is it Hobbsy the tutor from my youth?
Halt the train, Lord Broghill. Halt this carriage.

HOBBES: Loving Returnéd Lord,
I never thought to be remembered, only to stand as you pass and express my heart's bursting joy at your return to govern England a Sovereign, and any man will tell you I daren't stop praying for the King's return, and even kept up my hand at arguing for assent and no divided power. Today my prayers are answered.

CHARLES: Is this the same old man?
My memory says Hobbes was not so pious,
And never talked of peace, but would want to war on every topic
And always be the last one shouting.
My memory's Hobbes was stacked with piss and vinegar.
Say, has age made you weary of biting words?

HOBBES: On the contrary, forgiving King,
Reasoned rhetoric and prudence remain my pounding weapons, even now
I feel invigorated in your new Kingdom; I am like to strike out against any treason I hear threatens your crown, I swear I will drown out all fanatics with the same fire you remember me for.

CHARLES: Never go soft. I must have you at court.
Meantime I grant you a stipend. A pension. Take note.

HOBBES: The King's kindness is abundant.

CHARLES: Twenty-five pound a year, hang on old man, I will have you at court, a bear to be baited, share your thoughts to amuse, and compare them to my own. Move on.

HOBBES: I await your order to service, with my breath held in, and stand at the ready to do your bidding in this new Christened, peaceful land.

CHARLES: Thanks, move on.

A flourish, CHARLES moves on.

BLACK: Success?

HOBBES: He loves me.

ROTTEN: Could you guess his mind as to the theatres?

HOBBES: You were right my dearest Black. My warrior's pose is the most memorable. The King wants me to get hard. He wills to escalate my war on Deceivers, surge them with my superior truth.

HOBBES, ROTTEN and BLACK exit.

WILKINS: It will take more than small gifts to earn a unit of this King's kindness, A unit goes to Hobbes, our enemy. This lascivious King is giving laurels to a presumed Atheist who lived peacefully underneath that ruler yonder piked. Now our worship should be out in the open and our industry rewarded, we should not be begging in line behind a senile demon whose unstable loyalty will surely lead to a war of all against all.

TRANSITION.

HOOKE: (*Alone.*) A man can buy my hands, borrow my eyes, he can pay for my time and command my legs to stand in his lab for however long he likes, but never get my secrets. My keen mind isn't loaned to anyone or bought, what I wrought up here is mine alone, will be signed by me, and all the while I do this labor I will be thinking of a thousand schemes to advance, two million achievements and inventions, and as long as I stoop, which will be until I die, in front of these proper choir boys and learned academes, and do the dance a droopy not-so-pretty boy from the Isle of Wight must do in front of men like that: I'll have money. Money to build my own machines much beyond what these jacking hacks with heavier, velveteen pockets could ever dream up. See I have a code I write in that only I know, I am so careful to keep my special revelations hidden, and play show-and-tell-share-alike with the other boys on their lower level; on any level I'm sure to run circles about them, hunch or no.

2.1

BLACK and ROTTEN are holding scrolls.

ROTTEN: What is the meaning of this play? It's ranting shit.
　　It is a just a list of fussy mental tumbles,
　　Arrogant rating, and this quite thick obscure dialogue,
　　If you can call it that,
　　Like some froward young man's uppity Punch play,
　　Where he plays Punch,
　　And the whole play is a cascade of landing blows
　　All thrown by Punch, aggrandizing the Puppeteer
　　At the expense of a woefully underwritten Judy.

BLACK: Daniel this is an experiment.

HOBBES: It is not an experiment. It is against experiments. What have I said?

BLACK: It is a certain trial for him—one moment—to convey your political
　　frame.

HOBBES: You have utterly misunderstood the story of the tract.
　　It is a classical dialogue, you are on the border of illiterate actors.
　　I am against any politics other than my own solution on sovereignty.
　　If you can't get that right I'm walking out.

BLACK: Thomas, you will stay and patiently forgive our inferior performer's
　　syntax and acknowledge you know nothing about conveying meaning in
　　front of crowds with voice and body.

HOBBES: Don't I walk and talk?

BLACK: Daniel—forgive all metaphors and stay author—
　　Daniel you are misunderstanding the scroll here.
　　The idea, I believe, is to blend, say, the town-cryer's style
　　With the impression of character, and interrupt their assembly.
　　We will be like a messenger, arrive suddenly,
　　Then capture all attention with our raw searing cry.

ROTTEN: We will be arrested.

BLACK: Our playing will determine that.
We might be arrested.
But if we deliver the message in a brief attack and flee—

HOBBES: How brief?

BLACK: We may outrun any soldiers they could call on.

HOBBES: How brief do you mean?

ROTTEN: This scroll is an evening lecture, we can't do all of it.

BLACK: We must cut it down to nothing more than one half a quarter of an hour.

HOBBES: One half a quarter? I'm walking out.

BLACK: Stop and imagine, those few minutes, if that, after we have interrupted them, their attention will be rapt, they will be in shock, and listen so closely.

HOBBES: The purpose in the tract is the utter humiliation of their Satanic faction. Utter humiliation, in order to be utter, cannot be truncated.

BLACK: But you have sent your detailed critique in pamphlet form to Robert Boyle and he replies not. In this our disrupting version the cry of injustice buried in your words must ring out in moments, not upon meditation.

HOBBES: It is a polite dialectic between teacher and student, the purpose: to instruct.

ROTTEN: But your Boyle in the scroll here is not worth the attack.
There is no play in a villain that loses every exchange at every juncture.
The Boyle I know wins men over instantly.

HOBBES: The purpose is not to make my enemy seem reasonable.

ROTTEN: But you must build Boyle up in order to tear him down.

BLACK: Okay, we will leave aside discussion of the big themes and hear aloud the moment our two totems, Hobbes and Boyle, meet.

ROTTEN: At a rock somewhere. A. sitting on a rock. B. arrives at the rock.
Where is this rock?

HOBBES: Doesn't matter.

ROTTEN: It is some reference to Ancient Rome?

HOBBES: No.

ROTTEN: Well why not have them meet on a specific street? And I'll say the
name of the street we meet on, so the crowd will recognize one of the words
in your play early on.

BLACK: Rotten, with apologies, in this guerilla style,
I suspect location is somewhat irrelevant.

ROTTEN: I'm trying to help him.

BLACK: I will read the first line. 'I see you as I wished.'

ROTTEN: He sees me as he wished, but why am I arriving?

BLACK: Read your line.

ROTTEN: 'And I am glad to hear you, for indeed I see nothing, since the
brightness of very clear days blinds me.' Days blinds me?

HOBBES: There you might hold up your hand as if to shield your eyes.

BLACK: We will determine that later, read on.

ROTTEN: Why not the brightness of this day? Not all days.

HOBBES: Because whenever things are clear the experimenter is blind.
Pause after days, 'very clear days…blinds me' and it will work.

ROTTEN: Is that how he wishes us to say it? Sir author, this is adaptation for
the stage.

BLACK: But not the stage.

ROTTEN: You would be braver to leave the playing style to us,
So we can make your meaning nicer.

BLACK: Mr. Hobbes, good author, instruct me how speak your doppleganger's
line, this Oracle of Philosophy.

HOBBES: Ah Hobbes' words, pronounce this way: 'Kneel by me, until that
excessive motion in your organ of vision settles.'

ROTTEN: Author let him say 'eye' for 'organ of vision,' the common word is more poetic.

BLACK: There is something in that.

ROTTEN: What?

BLACK: His reading of it.

ROTTEN: That wooden style?

BLACK: That wooden-ness though, is so natural. It is better suited to the bluntness of the form. The blunter the interruption, the more unfamiliar the style, the closer they will listen to his scorching critique, if the playing is too fluid, as yours was always renowned to be—

ROTTEN: Thank you.

BLACK: It will be but familiar farce. We must imitate his stilted and authentic style in our portrayal. Borrow from life to sabotage life.

HOBBES: I am glad you give your assent to me.

BLACK: Or braver still: Why not send Mr. Hobbes on as himself?

HOBBES: What do you mean?

ROTTEN: Am I still Boyle?

BLACK: You will perform with Mr. Rotten.

HOBBES: I can't be seen to have initiated this Black. We agreed. If you are arrested I will rescue you, but you must not confess I was party to the spectacle, only say that you are renegade admirers of mine delivering an oral lecture that went somewhat awry.

BLACK: That plan can remain with you playing the part. You will be disguised. No one there will know Hobbes is behind the play.

HOBBES: Disguised as who?

BLACK: Disguised as Hobbes. The perfect disguise. For who would disguise himself as himself? Wear this false beard. Who better than you? Your casual oratory honed in bars, and your passionate attachment to the material is all the style we'll need to steal their ears, as long as you are prepared to run.

HOBBES: Will we run off? Can't we march off when the oratory is complete? That is more dignified.

BLACK: I mean if soldiers are called.

HOBBES: Soldiers of this crown won't arrest me for expressing my mind in public. But in disguise, I suppose, it is a disturbance. If soldiers come, I can run.

ROTTEN: If ever I wished to run off at the end of a performance, this is the one.

BLACK: I will be a patsy in the crowd, and shout out praise to buy you more time. Now, we will cut down your scroll, rehearse our disruption, Humiliate the Gresham Group at their very next public meeting, And make their public into yours.

2.2

Outside the King's Chamber.

WILKINS: Look at my hair for me, say is it straight.

WILLIS: It is straight. And mine?

WILKINS: Fine.

WILLIS: I am happy to meet a real King after all these years.

WALLIS: I am cold. When will that door open?

A CAVALIER strides by.

WILKINS: Here is a feathered guard. Good day noble Lord.

CAVALIER: Waiting for his majesty?

WILLIS: We are.

CAVALIER: How long have you stood here?

WALLIS: A long time.

WILKINS: Which is no complaint.

WILLIS: Not at all.

WILKINS: In exchange for the privilege.

WILLIS: It is a privilege.

CAVALIER: I get it. (*Exit.*)

WILLIS: You are too sycophantic John.

WILKINS: What do you mean?

WALLIS: He means that flattery is a subtle art and not so blunt.
    To compliment a King inartfully is the same as insulting him.

WILLIS: I have been in need of a chamber pot for the last hour.

WILKINS: The moment you go the door will open.

WALLIS: This is the moment to caution Charles about Thomas Hobbes. I will
    do it.

WILKINS: No John no words of caution for the King. We must win his love.

WALLIS: Then after we win his love I will mention it.

WILKINS: Mentioning enemies straight away will wrangle the King. He has
    given Hobbes a pension, and given us nothing, so: Patience, Gentle John.

WILLIS: Remember Boyle doesn't want beef.

WALLIS: Any charter we achieve must exclude Hobbes. That is true.
    I won't lie to my Sovereign. Reigning Hobbes in is what we want.

WILKINS: Lying is wrong, but revealing all is impolitic,
    Stick to the gift script today John, Hobbes' time will come.

WILLIS: What if the King is naked when the door opens?

WALLIS: As an accident? We'll shield our eyes.

    BROGHILL enters.

BROGHILL: He means on purpose, and possibly he will be.
    This King gets wet.
    We can't know how many actresses he has rutted with today.
    He may admit us with one still glistening in the bed beside him.
    That is the French way.

Whatever is behind that door you must appear unmoved.

WILKINS: He won't be naked.

BROGHILL: The king may have ejaculated just here. Anywhere around here.

WALLIS: I can't believe it.

WILKINS: Thank you for this Roger. It means so much.

BROGHILL: Where are your gifts?

WILKINS: The gifts are metaphors good Lord.
The gift of our ingenuity, we will explain it all to the King.

BROGHILL: Oh. But you haven't got long. Are you asking for money?

WILKINS: For a charter.

BROGHIL: I remember. Are you doing a demonstration?

WIKLINS: A presentation.

BROGHILL: Oh. (*Something slides away.*) Here is the door.
Be stony-faced good Greshamites. Appear unmoved.

CHARLES: Alright what's this?

CAVALIER: Your majesty, Lord Broghill, Roger Boyle.

CHARLES: Roger.

CAVALIER: And friends.

CHARLES: Come in. How is the garrison at Cork?

BROGHILL: Strongly held. Your majesty a thousand thanks.
Allow me to introduce John Wilkins, John Wallis, and Thomas Willis.
The industry of these men has come to my attention, and their gifts, their grace, and information may prove useful to you and your State.

WILKINS: Majesty, on behalf of our entire Gresham Group,
We come bearing three gifts:
Ingenuity, Prosperity, and Exclusivity, to you.

WILLIS: Ingenuity: All the men in our group—

CHARLES: This is a presentation?

WILKINS: Yes your majesty.

WILLIS: —Are independent gentlemen of means and learning.
We build, we solve, we grow and sew the seeds of Progress, offering
sensible attacks on the toughest problems and elegant solutions, to brighten
England's blinking bitter darkness.

WALLIS: Prosperity the second gift is promised by our patent system.

CHARLES: Now he speaks.

WALLIS: Inventions can be vetted, publications reviewed by noble peers, and
England's glories publicized and patented across the continent. Our group,
numbering fifty-five spotless royal loyals, accepted no grant or coat from
Cromwell. Our law of falling bodies can make this nation strong with
cannon ball improvements.

CHARLES: Oh please no more war.

WILKINS: We know your very forward and enlightened attitude toward time,
which we will soon standardize, and your experiments through telescopes,
which we wish to publish and add to our annuals, The King's Discoveries,
Moons Crowned, all for you.

CHARLES: Yes I have discovered certain things gazing at the stars that should
be shared with my people.

WILKINS: And just to say, Exclusivity is the third gift: Our group's unflagging
pledge to give over all our ingenuities gratis to the state.

CHARLES: Yes. Wonderful. Three promises, you call gifts. I commend your
loyalty.

WILKINS: There was a watch we gave you, before the coronation, a small gift of
friendship we hope you enjoy…ed?

CHARLES: Yes I collect them. Your group is good. Anything else?

WILKINS: Gracious King might we continue our operations with your blessing
and support? A charter for our group, to seal our improvements with your
royal wax?

CHARLES: Do you need that? Are you not better off as independent men of
  means?

WALLIS: Independence is vain, Majesty, and cannot be trusted.
  When rewards go to the State men labor better and for a greater good.
  It is the old Philosophers who serve themselves for vain glory alone.

CHARLES: Philosophers of old or old ones in our midst? I miss your meaning.

WALLIS: I'd be a liar if I said there weren't opponents in our field of knowledge.

WILKINS: But we wish no dispute with any citizen of yours.

CHARLES: Enemies are interesting. Speak.

WALLIS: Your majesty. I am a teacher—

WILKINS: John.

WALLIS:—and a preacher. I work for Country, King, and Kind. But I am
  plagued constantly by cross and lurid attacks lobbed by Mr. Thomas Hobbes.

CHARLES: A friend of mine. The worse for you.
  There is some bickering between you and that old man?
  He makes me laugh.

WILKINS: Oh he makes all of us laugh. He is a gay and not-yet-forgotten old
  father of some no-doubt important part of older knowledge growing up.

WALLIS: Who is past time retiring, and still walking when he should be arming
  a chair, still chanting when he should be idly admiring the exhilarating
  progress of younger men.

CHARLES: He is not ready to retire his store of wisdom.

WILKINS: Nor should he, nor should any explorer in Nature be dampened in
  your new Christened Kingdom.

WALLIS: Majesty we aim to correct the course bent by any untender followers
  of this scientific faith, and quiet those friends whose rabbling style is wont to
  disturb the peace.

CHARLES: Roger you are a Lord. Why are you linked with these men? Only for
  your brother?

BROGHILL: Not only Sovereign, though my admiration for that gentle creature does reach beyond fraternity. I love my brother dearly, and believe in his missioning work. Their Industry seems right for your time. As to the rest; In truth, I'd say, a rancorous friend may cancel out ten valued champions, Your majesty.

CHARLES: These preeners and schemers are not right for me. Send them away. (*BROGHILL takes them out.*) England needn't be so radically different in every detail. We need older faces too.
I recognize an opportunity spreader when I see three.
I know because I am Opportunity's favorite whore.
I fall upwards into every opportunity I find, doing somersaults.
These bookish men stumble horribly.
Perhaps the King himself should be the only licensed Philosopher in the land.
I'll look into that.

TRANSITION

WILKINS: What have you done John? Made us enemies with the King?

BROGHILL: That went poorly.

WALLIS: We should prove our superiority to him, not lobby like puppies, John. It was your idea to walk in with three invisible gifts.

WILLIS: Wallis is right. We must set a demonstration for the King to prove our worth.

BROGHILL: Why have you lashed out against Thomas Hobbes? He is Charles' harmless court jester. It made you seem so petty.

WALLIS: He is a jester that whispers in the King's ear what philosophy should be, he curses me, and rails against your brother too.

BROGHILL: My brother no. He does not dispute.

WALLIS: But Hobbes is wily bully. He lashes out unprovoked for vanity. He calls your brother a deceiver and a Satanic spawn Roger.

BROGHILL: Bring me evidence. Set your demonstration day.
Put your visible gifts on display. I will endeavor to bring the King again.

TRANSITION

WALDORF: That's my printing press shut down.

STATLER: Oh no man.

WALDORF: Closed by the King. Only four large shops are blessed with licenses and all the rest revoked. What will I do? Now it is illegal to ply my trade. Are words so dangerous to this Restoration that a simple shop keeper must be shut out? You and I are useless in this world. All the old ways are being trampled. Today another Tyrant is born in England, and sitting in the highest seat.

2.3

At BOYLE's laboratory.

BOYLE: These are shocking drawings Robert.

HOOKE: Thank you Virtuoso. Not every man can own or gaze through a microscope, but they may see a perfect drawing of what has been seen.

BOYLE: This must be published.

WILLIS: Will people believe this is a flea seen up close?
    It looks like the most horrible bottom-crawling ocean monster.

BOYLE: Brother Wilkins take this manuscript to the finest printer, to make templates. Use the master inker to reproduce these drawings. We will present the maiden version of your remarkable book to the King at next week's public demonstration. He will be the first to see it, then copies will be sold at the shop at the Bell.

WILKINS: It must be dedicated to the King.
    As secretary I can write the dedication and save you the trouble.

HOOKE: I have written a dedication to the King.

WILKINS: That is fine, but there is a format in which one writes to the King which you may not be familiar with.

HOOKE gets it from COX.

HOOKE: I have written it well, listen:
    'TO THE KING—Sir, I do here most humbly lay this small present at your Majesties Royal feet. And though it comes accompany'd with two

disadvantages, the meanness of the Author, and of the Subject, yet in both I am encouraged by the greatness of your Mercy and your forward mind…'

WILKINS: You have captured the format I think.

BOYLE: England will be flooded with our finest achievements.

WILLIS: I have a marvelous dissected specimen, and a meridian of the brain I have named. That could be announced for the King.

WILKINS: What meridian?

WILLIS: I call it the Circle of Willis.

BOYLE: A displayed brain may be too mean a thing to show at our first Royal look. We must present our most thrilling and plainly visible experiments to the Sovereign, so he may see how we command the crowd and bring those assembled into harmonious agreement.

WILKINS: Thomas you may name that meridian but not announce it at this important meeting. Likewise, your geometry, John, will be reserved.

WALLIS: I am happy to leave laymen out my geometry. It cannot be translated to the masses.

BOYLE: What experiment will proceed the air-pump?

WILKINS: The pump will be the finale then?

HOOKE: Surely. But we must select some lesser but no less impressive demonstration to warm them up. Why not show my collection of ancient shells and share my conjecture on the long dead bugs that appear to be frozen in the stone.

BOYLE: Not those Robert.

WILLIS: What of our solutions for disease? We tell the King that lives can be prolonged by our advancing medicine.

HOOKE: Or attach a catalogue of our patented improvements, for microscopes.

WILKINS: It is telescopes the King most enjoys.

WALLIS: Can we not drop cannon balls from the roof as the King arrives?

In honor of Galileo's achievement at Pisa. Maybe drop them in time with music?

BOYLE: We must invite parts of the public that have never seen our show before,
So the wonderment if fresh in the room, new in front of the King,
So we are seen to please those outside our sphere.

WILLIS: Which experiment inside the air-pump will be the finale?

HOOKE: Whichever one the Virtuoso chooses.

WILKINS: It will be a reliable one I hope, and not one of those that sometimes fails, or needs to be reset five times, by you.

HOOKE: Mr. Secretary my pump is perfected. It squeezes and presses Aire perfectly. The valves are perfect. I have master-pieced this machine for Boyle so thoroughly—Maybe Mr. Secretary you don't understand that this is not yesterday's pump. Many men think hard about tomorrow, but always end up picturing another yesterday. Look hard Secretary, my stop-cock is the securest, on earth, ever created. Even in a degraded state Boyle's machine is the most miraculous.

WILKINS: Even the most perfect pneumatic engine must work perfectly in front of a King, or be imperiled Young Hooke.

BOYLE: You argue too sternly for the things you love Robert.
This group must need the King, and will wish hard to capture his heart.
But the true quest here does not belong to us. Our earthly obstacles now are no match for the growing light. Even if we are laughed off in our short lives, this light will grow. We are but the ember at it's lowest ebb, glowing barely in the dark. The light after us, with God's blessing, with grow to blind.

HOOKE: Wilkins look, I have sealed all the leaks. Hear that high-pitched whistle? The final hole. When I smear this cement in it, the engine will be silent. No more Aire whistles through. A white hot coal goes almost cold in half as many strokes, birds expire and are revived repeatedly in minutes. Mercury sails up and down in the barometer now each and every time I operate this pump. There will be no waiting around, no focus on my preparations. I will be commanding Aire in mere moments on the stage. The Virtuoso will speak straight away, from his powerful observing position, and do the purest version of our patter for the King and crowd—

BOYLE/HOOKE: 'When a man is lawful master to his senses, keen, patient, and true—

HOOKE: —'Then the true miracle of Nature can be observed and known.' Just like that. Go ahead Virtuoso.

BOYLE: No more rehearsal.

WILKINS: But, young Robert, if your engine is so advanced, why not leave it to your younger assistant to do that manual labor, and reserve a place on the floor for yourself among the other worthy Gentlemen?

COX: What you say is true Robert, the engine is now easy enough for me operate.

HOOKE: But in the event that it needs some special or immediate attention, in front of the king, my hands should be close.

BOYLE: No more. We will fall to our preparations, all.

Exit all but BOYLE and WILKINS.

WILKINS: Virtuoso your assistant's book is rife with the very conjecture and guessing you have sought to quash.

BOYLE: I am tormented by the inadequacy of words,
And Hooke does offend, but in his drawings I see God.
So we will forgive him here, and leave his sometime mad conjectures in.

2.4

Outside Gresham College

HOBBES: I see it now. I see it all. Reading will vanish, the written word will fall to English, that's Latin gone. Now we move our idea war to the performing front. I hear it too, crowds roaring, carrying us out on their shoulders.

ROTTEN: I had real danger across my hide under Cromwell Black,
I want to know our out.

BLACK: But my disguise is perfect, Rotten, have no doubt.

HOBBES: What will be my signal to emerge?

ROTTEN: You will hear my voice from your hiding place.

HOBBES: Say it loud.

ROTTEN: I may linger in my opening moment, as it is my only solo,
    So don't emerge before the proper cue.

BLACK: But not too late.

HOBBES: Upon my mark. I've got it.

TRANSITION

STATLER: To appear before the King, even as an assistant, is a special day for you.
    So I thought you'd need a coat.

COX: No uncle, I have these clothes.

STATLER: Something smart to wear. So when the king spots you,
    He will see a small gentleman, and not some shoe shining boy.

COX: If we are successful in our endeavor today, I will be employed by a Royal
    ensemble. And if I pay my dues, I can remain on their roster forever. My life
    has begun. (*COX puts on the coat.*)
    I do feel proud in it. Does it look proud?

STATLER: It looks like Progress. Bright boy. The new world is not so new to you.

COX: Go inside uncle. This coat is fab.

STATLER exits.

WALDORF catches COX.

WALDORF: You need to give your real father some gold to hold son.

COX: Are you coming in to watch?

WALDORF: I want you to know I don't need the gold. I just need to hold it.

COX: I can't prop you up father, why haven't you saved?

WALDORF: How dare you speak to me like that? How double dare you son?
    You want a slap?

COX: I'm paying fees to the group now. I can't give you more money.

WALDORF: That's real funny to me. More money? I'm not in debt to you. This
    is you feeling yourself because you think you're strong. You're not strong

son. I'm not even sure you could take me in a fight, only that you've got everything to prove so you'd probably fight dirty.

COX: I need to save my gold and find a wife.

WALDORF: You're a tinker little cracker, what makes you think you'll find a wife?

COX: I'm due to be a big man in science dad. Come inside if you wish. (*He exits.*)

TRANSITION

CHARLES: Hold back a moment Lord Broghill. Late arrival is more powerful. It makes men meditate on how much they love you, and fear you will not come. Let them creep up close to the cliff of their adoration, so that my arrival pushes them over. They are so stiffly virginal and hopeless devoted to me, I confess I like to see them squirm.

TRANSITION

BROGHILL: (*Solo.*) See this warrant in my hand?
   Can we call it Progress when the gentle and the mild are insulted and attacked,
   And all attempts at Peace are thwarted and delayed by braying bullies
   Spraying hateful lies, sending strikes against our most vulnerable civilians?
   This Hobbes slanders my brother and by extension, me.
   He is blunt and drags up the past, his pose is of the past,
   Plus his black book is full of black ticks to condemn every man a traitor.
   I did what I had to, under Cromwell's nightmare reign.
   My necessary indiscretions have been blotted
   But this indiscreet blaster is liable to spill.
   He doesn't know the brother Boyle I am,
   No oath of softly softly ever crossed my lips,
   And Hobbes has met his match at splitting up The Self:
   There's always two of me for any Civil War occasion,
   And one of them is guaranteed to stand next to the winner.
   So I say Leviathan inspired Levelers—implying Hobbes conspired too—
   This warrant brought to parliament will get his book examined
   And all his papers tossed, to figure out the heresy
   And any treason on his books, have him censored, or better burned.
   Did Hobbes love Levelers? I think not.

Hobbes argues for one strong leader,
The Levelers screamed there should be none.
But Hobbes disdain for Divine Rights lines up fine with Levelers,
And he never condemned their sect in print. Too late Thom.
You will be crinkled tinsel underneath my heel, your twinkle will into mud,
thud, hater, yield.

2.5

Inside Gresham college. Many assembled. HOOKE *is finishing an experiment with light.*

WALDORF: Yup I've seen this one already.

STATLER: You haven't seen the pneumatic engine.

WALLIS: Where is the King?

WILLIS cues applause.

STATLER: (*To NEWTON.*) I remember when they did these sorts of things in backrooms. Do you remember that?

NEWTON: No.

WALLIS: (*To STATLER.*) Progress is swift.

WALDORF: I've seen this one.

WILKINS: Welcome Ladies and Gentlemen. My name again is John Wilkins. We are going to begin again in just a moment. And yes, the King will come. But you assembled here, true and learned witnesses, cherished collaborators and friends, are all the hearts and minds we need to demonstrate out our most humble and ingenious offerings. In just a few moments, the Circle of Willis.

HOOKE: (*Aside.*) You were kind to include Thom's brain.

BOYLE: (*Aside.*) Is everything prepared?

HOOKE: Yes Virtuoso, but we must hold our engine until the King arrives.

COX: Robert let me standby on stage. If there are any sudden leaks you'll need four hands to save her.

HOOKE: You won't fit in the frame Chris, stand upstage as we arranged.

NEWTON: (*To WALLIS.*) My love is maths.

WALLIS: Maths are the highest art. Trust me when I say there are deeper calculations that anchor all this showy stuff.

NEWTON: I just began at Cambridge but they still teach Aristotle. I know more Kepler than the lecturer and I'm just 18.

WALLIS: Shame, I'm back to Oxford. You'll be joining this Group soon enough Isaac. Attending these meetings is a good start.

NEWTON: I don't know.

WALDORF: (*To STATLER.*) You are the grandfather behind my boy's rise. But when he falls who will catch him?

STATLER: There is no falling anymore, only journeys upward.

WILKINS: And without further delay: Doctor Thomas Willis.
From your ovation I know you know the Good Doctor; most renowned for raising the dead. Every gentleman wants to see this anatomy of a man, not a miracle-worker, no, his huge brain saves lives. Thomas, before your demonstration, tell the story.

WILLIS: I think everyone here knows the story. A hanged woman in a box arrived at my practice. At first, we assumed that she was dead, but assumption fell away when I felt that she was warm. I instantly fell and kissed her full of Aire—

CAVALIER: The King is come!

WILKINS: Prayer works.

BROGHILL: His majesty, Charles Stuart!

WILLIS: Long live the King!

ALL: Long live the King! Long live the King.

CHARLES: Sorry I'm tardy. Carry on as if I weren't here.

WILKINS: Your majesty, I am John Wilkins, secretary for this Group, Astronomy's my art. Allow me to remind you of the chief Virtuosi in our sphere. Doctor Thomas Willis, Neurologist.

CHARLES: I never heard that word before.

WILLIS: I coined it, Majesty.

WILKINS: The Bishop John Wallis, Geometry.

WALLIS: Your majesty.

WILKINS: And the Honorable Robert Boyle.

CHARLES: Wave to your brother Roger.

BROGHILL: His Sacrosanctity is as Pure as his Science, Majesty.

WILKINS: Tardiness is nothing in this room Sovereign. This show of science, our cascade of facts, never ceases, it is in every waking walking moment of our work. And, as we all said at The Coronation, King, your timing is perfect. Fate you should arrive now, in time to witness our most glorious mechanical achievement, Robert Boyle's Pneumatic Engine. At once.

HOOKE fires up the engine. WILLIS pushed aside.

BOYLE: Fact. Plain thing from nature. Fact: A fruit, falls, no picking. Intelligent Cause is all around us, and the Laws of Life are Miracles. Miracles once, were Mythologies, passed along by Men. Now miracles are Laws of Nature, and we need take no man's word. We Virtuosi may step away, lift our hands, but these repeating Miracles sustain. These will be confirmed by All after our deaths, where our aim was true. Where we err, let that be overturned instantly by better facts in future, let facts grow, build around them, let them feed, nurse the light, condemn all darkness which threatens the pansophic transcendence of man.

WALDORF: What's pansophic mean?

STATLER: He means he is Pansophia, Universe and Wisdom wedded.

WALDORF: And what's a vacuum?

STATLER: Nothing.

BOYLE: But leave aside our mission and my imperfect words
And give your witness now to the distinct, transparent and unanimously observed, plain property called
The Spring in Aire:

HOOKE is pumping.

BOYLE: Now when a man is lawful master onto his Senses, keen patient and true—

ROTTEN enters.

ROTTEN: I am the Spirit of the Aire! The Spirit of the Aire,
I'm facing judgment here,
From a spry old seer:
The Oracle of Philosophy!

HOBBES emerges dressed as the Oracle of Philosophy. BLACK enters the hall disguised as a soldier.

HOBBES: I see you as I wished.

ROTTEN: Help me, I see nothing, for the brightness of clear days does blind.

HOBBES: Stop searching, accept my way, and Sight is what you'll find.

ROTTEN: But high up here, my mind is scared, upon your shade-less perch.

HOBBES: Yes you prefer it where it's dimmer, inside your secret church.

ROTTEN: But from our lab we see the world the way our God designed it.

HOBBES: God's design will never change, your science can't refine it.

ROTTEN: That is correct but doesn't God approve of all our jargon?

HOBBES: God's opinion we cannot know, but Man should stick with Latin.

ROTTEN: That is true, but experiments are a new way to be Wise.

HOBBES: But Experience, the wiser way, burns through your thin disguise.

ROTTEN: But our Experiments have lately shown the Vacuum to be true.

HOBBES: Nature hates a Vacuum Sir, the absence here is You.

ROTTEN: But our Machines make us the very newest Kings of Science—

WILLIS: Tear down this treason, it is no part of our show.

BROGHILL: Take these graceless hecklers out. (*To BLACK.*) Soldier there.

ROTTEN: By what authority would any challenge the Oracle of Philosophy?

95

BROGHILL: By authority of the King. (*To BLACK.*) Solider there, grab that fool. Soldier.

CHARLES: A Somewhat witty act of terror.

BROGHILL: Soldier what are you good for?

HOBBES sees the King.

HOBBES: Charlie my God forgive this…

BLACK shackles ROTTEN.

BROGHILL: Put them in the stocks out front.

CHARLES: Does anyone in your group wish to answer this attack? Unmask the Oracle there and let him hear retort.

WILKINS: Your majesty we want not to duel with words.

HOBBES: I am not a disrupting player. I am Thomas Hobbes.

CHARLES: Oh no old bear, what rude imposition is this?

HOBBES: Upright King, these men are my enemies. Let me explain the origin of my quarrel.

BOYLE: We heard your words cruel man, listen to me. Wisdom must be Universal.

HOBBES: Sovereign will this priest of the new snatch philosophy for himself?

BOYLE: There can be no leading luminary, no lone holder of the light.

HOBBES: What light is here? I see an empty promise on your altar.

BOYLE: Your model of dispute is obsolete.

HOBBES: You mean to soothe us with blind hubris.

BOYLE: You are the animus man inside us all.

HOBBES: You warp the minds and mine the purses.

BOYLE: Man is flawed.

HOBBES: While making men of sense stare at whore's machines.

BOYLE: We wish to transcend your teeming insect war.

HOBBES: It is a tinker's parody of beauty.

BOYLE: Trade it for a bird's casual congress with the Aire.

HOBBES: Parody perverse enough to make men scream 'Miracle!'

BOYLE: For birds never argued amongst themselves the way to fly.

HOBBES: What answers do you have to other things?

BOYLE: They took that power together from heaven.

HOBBES: What soil is on the moon? What mover makes the earth inhale?

BOYLE: A union of minds will settle these things in time.

HOBBES: Why tides? What are roots? What is blushing?

BOYLE: Scripture, Myth, Prophecy and Legend tell Humanity Light wins in
the End. Light will banish all Darkness.

HOBBES: Oh raven-eyed terror, it won't. Darkness is always at the end.

BOYLE: Wolf! Dogmatic sheer through all your non-destructible bones.
Cast your harsh light off our peaceful scene, father of Atheists.

HOBBES: Not a true peaceful scene is it? War! Wrought by this cursed machine
and the wizard standing next to her. And that gargoyle seed right there.
Mercy Sovereign.

CHARLES: Poor old man, fall to prayers.
You are unstrung fallen stranger.
You are dangling; here's me ready to cut you loose.
You make it hard old man. Your fire is tempting and sexy hot. But the
blockage in your heart is too traumatic for our future.
We need peace, old crazy, peace, you grey beast. This world wipes you off at
the finish, that's Fate.
We won't remember you. This is the last kiss.
Mwah silver gorilla, folly is your shroud.

BROGHILL: My lord, in good time.
A bill is here. Signed by several men.
To investigate out of Hobbes his much suspected sedition

97

And the same heresy enumerated here.

CHARLES: Walk away.

HOBBES: I am more than abandoned.
    My life's work will be evidence against me.
    Fear, my twin, returns. (*Exits.*)

WALLIS: (*To HOBBES.*) I will dedicate my life to stalling your pension, die in poverty devourer of minds, beast.

BROGHILL: Drag out his conspirator. Hold, soldier there. I recognize your face. Next to that knave's face it is familiar. That man is part of this plot. Unmask him. All actors in the stocks.

CAVALIER takes ROTTEN and BLACK away.

CHARLES: Congratulations Gentle Gresham, your display is fine. The intrusion is forgiven. And by the power invested in me I anoint you to be the Royal Society, to serve at my pleasure here forth.

BOYLE:(*Aside.*) I have never brimmed with so much hate.
    My voice is hoarse, my fingers numb.
    This quaking heart is sore.
    I banish feeling hence.
    It murders all joy.
    It scars my soul.
    Disappear.
    Robert.
    Fly.

2.6

HOBBES is seen in his study, burning papers and notes. There is a Great Fire in London. People form bucket-lines, belongings are rescued, bodies are passed to safety. ROTTEN and BLACK escape from prison. CHARLES surveys the wreckage.

2.7

The Tragedy of Robert Hooke.

HOOKE: London's more than scalded, more than scolded. God Gomorrah'ed us here,
  He threw our city's solar plexus into cleansing fire as kindling. London burned.
  But why am I surveying a flattened smoldering scar from this protected perch?
  Well the fire stopped just there, where I can just about lob a stone, there it stopped.
  The Royal Society is saved by God, and this place, where I live, as it is a new Zero Ground on the border of disaster's centre, the Corporation of London has moved in, to begin rebuilding. But what do corporations know about reconstruction? They've never seen an instant adept like me, I am a better sketcher than all their drafters squared, now I'm in charge. Architecture I pick up in moments, it's not even a science. Now I know why our city is so tangled; builders never had access to a genius cluster like this. I will rebuild London on a grid. Beautiful rational, and bring broader fame to this group. Now that my patron has retired from public life, I can guide a new even more experimental program, overturn more clogging dogma, and clear the way for me. Don't correct my stoop in the frame, I want to be remembered anon in the same shape my fame on earth was first known, no smudges.

BUILDERS: Hey Robert! Alright Mate?

HOOKE: Builders that love me tip hats. Purged twice today, giddy,
  Took sulfur and tincture of steel.

WILKINS: Master Newton, genius young Cambridge Don,
  We embrace your calculus, I want you
  To send us anything, anything you're working on.

NEWTON: I never think to submit my proofs or thoughts to any group.

I don't have time to stop and explain it all.
But this Wilkins is persistent,
I will mention my paper on light.

WILKINS: What of light?

NEWTON: That it is All colors.

WILKINS: Send it me.

NEWTON: And that it is particles.

WILKINS: Not waves?

NEWTON: An improvement on that Hooke book so adored in the past.

HOOKE: Light is particles? Pah! Light is a Wave.
So said I in my most famous book.

BUILDER: Which book is your most famous?

HOOKE: Why Micrografia! (*A cry of approval!*) Keep cheering!
Where I said Light was Waves!
Now our lame Royal store explores the nipping of every little yapping dog.
They are so lost without me if I ever miss a meeting,
They can't stage anything juicy without me,
Wilkins just reads his wicked correspondence aloud.

WILLIS: That was bloody boring.

WALLIS: I like when John reads letters.

WILKINS: Hooke is a neglecting cat in the street,
He only curls back home for milk. But when we need him
He's drawing building plans with Christopher Wren in our attic.

WALLIS: Living rent-free.

WILKINS: On our accounts.

WILLIS: The crowds come for him,
Not to hear the maths proofs or disputes you cook up.

WALLIS: Really? I find most of Hooke's rambling conjecture to be intolerable.

WILKINS: It is plain we need better Virtuosi than this disloyal, secret-keeping
low-born coiled shrub. With his supposed Spring watch, but no one can
peek inside?

WALLIS: Worse he shows it to the King alone. Or only Boyle.

HOOKE: The King saw my sea clock today. It is not yet perfected,
But will keep perfect time for at least two weeks while I build a better model.

CHARLES: It stopped.

WILKINS: That is patent hoarding for profit, not Progress for our Group
This Group I have given all my ribs to shape.
I have sacrificed all my pride for this thing I love.
But I can't cut loose our loafing members.
I can't call in debts for fear of mass resigning.
This pestilence and fire in England will depress science into a winter death.

HOOKE: Dr. Wilkins, I do apologize for dereliction in my duties, leaving
you without a proper experiment, for the first week in many months;
but dereliction is no excuse for you to invite amateurs under our tent to
summarize my work and then neglect to credit me. This Newton has copied
out my most famous book and added one little guessing quibble on top.

NEWTON: He copied his from Descartes, John. You asked me to report my
latest work. I had not expected to be spanked for this by your in-house
dogmatic, this wild man, that has done no advanced maths in his life and
raises both his hands against me. Is he your curator and stager of shows
or this group's authority on all ideas? If it is the later, I'll stay out of your
Society, and deliver my hard wrought calculations to a body friendlier and
less constrained by avarice and greed.

WILKINS: Please Isaac, hold my hand.
Say you will sometime share your ravishing maths with me alone.
Let me know what you know, from your perch of pure research far above.
Let me see what advances lay beyond this choking child society of mine.

HOOKE: I am convinced that Wilkins is against me, that he delivers my
blueprints to foreign agents, who reinvent my designs in their land and sell
the English patent back to Wilkins. So slow boiling designs of mine are
being plucked from my garden prematurely translated across borders and sold
back to cheating shifters in my own ensemble. I've no choice but to code my

proofs until we reincorporate this branch for Active scientists only and swear an oath of secrecy, to keep all discoveries undisclosed, seal these leaks. I take Spirit of Sal-Ammoniac with small beer at supper and barely sleep a wink.

NEWTON: I never hate to be alone.
I am content to stare into the sun for minutes,
Then make my room a cave for days
And watch the crystalline equations
That zoom and float across my lid's black curtain.
I re-draw them in the Cambridge gardens at night when I am foraging,
Math students guard them and pray against rain, clergy kids gawk and stare
Thinking 'What creature beyond all Reason
Landed here and dug in these celestial hieroglyphs?'
Stupid things. It was a creature of superior human reason
Writing in the language of God, Pure Mathematics.
One night I flew a kite with a red lantern attached,
For shame how the country people fast gave up the ghost and bowed.

HOOKE: Lately this Royal Society is a burdensome lamprey always at my side sucking. They work me like a dog presenting experiments weekly, whilst I've got thirty churches to design for a thick mint. Their paltry stipend and Royal flush equals me a slave in their reclining minds, the nerve, while they all idle at their one idea and present bi-monthly, I'm shucking once a week. Why am I weekly entertaining snoozing amateurs and giving away precious secrets to a wagging snake?

BUILDERS: Hey Robert Hooke, that monument you built is mint!

HOOKE: Cloudy morning, took a Wormwood Infusion and vomited thrice.
Napped and was refreshed. Wondered about the pores in trees.

WILLIS: You've been warned.

HOOKE: I am building Bedlam Thom. A dormitory for the Insane.
A corporate commission, double mint. They loved my monument.

WILLIS: Dance with the one that brought you Hooke. This nest is kindly laid for you. You use our name to prosper.

HOOKE: Christopher Wren is keeping up with me.
We share this London rebirth equally.
I love him, I trust him, but I do vet his sketches,

I'm at Garraways, and Childs, at Pasqua Rosee's Head
They stand a pint for me.
I am at the coffee houses like a Chinese chess master who plays fifty
opponents at once, juggling many games.
Ask any of the boys, Pif knows, Wal, Lodowick and Hain;
I'm with all my friends talking about flying wings, hydrostatics, helioscopes,
And my theory that the Earth's poles have shifted,
That the axis have been rearranged. I know it.

WILLIS: If you know it, show it.

HOOKE: Not yet.

WILLIS: Then let me tempt you, tempt the world,
   With a prize, five-hundred pounds to the man that proves
   Celestial Motion.

HOOKE: I have settled that.

WILLIS: Oh no. You know what I mean. Five-hundred pounds for the Real
   solution.

HOOKE: Dear master Newton: The reflecting telescope you sent us was most
   impressive, though it did begin to tarnish and flake after a few weeks.
   To wit, I have vastly improved your wonderful design, perfected, with the aid
   of Christopher Cox, who master-pieced a steel tube so true we could only
   stare at it together for long hours and polish it with tender fingers.

NEWTON: I've never been so insulted.

WILKINS: I'm sorry.

NEWTON: They'll never hear a word from me again.

WILKINS: Nonsense Virtuoso, your discoveries belong here.

NEWTON: Why is this man so vain, so incapable of seeing his own flaws?
   Am I not allowed to improve on Hooke's discoveries?
   Are his discoveries beyond reproach?

WILKINS: Look at him. He's a crooked bastard. He's always been all wrong.

NEWTON: Am I meant to stay off his turf? How is that possible when he pisses
   in every field, at pace, a few drops, here, a few drops there, I haven't the time

to finish it', 'It will be perfected anon!' He overuses a word that is so plainly opposite to him, he is imperfect in all ways. He is only a perfect dabbler, the very definition.

HOOKE: I Swallow iron and boiled milk to wake up my mind and scrape out the slime. On the Isle of Wight, I found twelve more stones with strange insects in relief, I know these are more than tricks of Nature.

WILLIS: They are tricks of Nature.

HOOKE: Tricks of nature? The shapes in seaside rocks are the very graves of creatures that have lived and died an age before our time, on coasts onetime located somewhere else in space, nameless floods and earthquakes too numerous for the Bible to list is the buried science of our earth!

WALLIS: I object to this insult. Your floods and shifting poles cannot be,
Without over-throwing all history sacred and profane.
This piercing vanity run amok would turn the World upside down.

HOOKE: John Wallis you've been at abstract graphs too long.
Most men in this room, and all residing on earth's equator know the world turns upside daily twice. Balance giddiness with poppy syrup and strong laxatives from Ben's Drugs.
Chris Cox defects to Newton's camp, I'll not speak to him again.

COX: You don't tell me who I work for, my hands belong to me.

WILKINS: Jagged Robert, sharp elbows and wild kicking concepts saying
That once mountains were valleys, deserts were rivers,
And a millennia of storms and quakes came before Eden's time;
That England itself is some volcano's purge from the ocean,
That ancient fish and bugs are imbedded in the bedrock earth,
Proving Earth has a backward reaching past, hanging here in space,
That animals are someway deformed over time by advantage,
Though nothing else sounds so absurd.

HOOKE: Sponsorship Royal or no is so much slower than rolling profit to underwrite man's careening Progress, we need to get paid, not give our blood away to some that never shed any. Boyle's vision is pious, but let me get mine. The prime-mover needs a heavy chest of drawers, I stack my gold underneath the bed. One hour of sleep leaves my eyes watery and sore. Wine keeps me awake.

NEWTON: I will credit the esteemed Mr. Robert Hooke for his grounding
contribution.
I will footnote that Robert Hooke for his thoughts.
I will endnote that Hooke among others.
I will sign Isaac alone.

HOOKE: Plotting my escape from this nest of vipers,
I need a higher scaffold to climb,
A secret group of the most industrious,
With no thieving Gentlemen and no Rosy Cross dues.
I need my own operation, I need out from under Wilkin's heel,
I've got too many idea to be wasting my time in this whipping post;
Curator? Twisting weekly my joints out of joint for a salary they are six
months behind in paying me? Cribbing all my words to fill their coffers?
Fie damned dogs! Get out of my face with that! I'll leave this place,
Be gone like Boyle, and float far above this well-financed grave.

NEWTON moves to the centre of the Royal Society.

BOYLE: Robert Hooke I remove my cloak from you, and do weep to imagine
the cold wind that will knife through your bones now. I dreamed of a boy
like you, a maybe virtuoso grown from organic soil, soprano singing choir
leader to inherit and one day own the light. But that was but a dream. On
earth real boys are vain. There is blood in their teeth. Dead floating jealousy
defines their eyes. Grit rings their nails. Speak to me not again stranger,
stay on if you can, but that wished for child of mine is stillborn. Villains
ruin wonder, they kill the sensitivity in sense, and neglect the pious part of
science. This thing we midwived was supposed to sing pure notes and be
sustained until the Rapture, but it will so soon be a din. Where drummers
drown out all the beauty, and screaming is the only way to be heard.

2.8

Outside a theatre.

ROTTEN: Mr. Boyle?

BOYLE: Who is it? Daniel. Last time I saw you, you were mocking.

ROTTEN: I have no hate for you Mr. Boyle. Come inside and see this play my
friend Black wrote. It is about your new Science. Or don't come in.

BOYLE: I won't. I must to prayer. I wouldn't be inside a theatre.

ROTTEN:It is the artist's charge to mock and tear down certain things to help
the people comprehend.

BOYLE: You mean condescend.

ROTTEN: I am a red-handed dreamer, caught here making more.
What can I say about dreams? They are my frontier.

BOYLE: Be cautious where you prostitute your soul,
You tall gold-blooming thing. Do you contrive those holes in your coat?
Or is that a costume?

ROTTEN: The holes are real but I wear them well.

BOYLE: All the wombs in my household are closed. I fade.
Cosmic mathematic grace beyond my patience and perception
Strides the earth before I've even gone, you see Daniel:
Our Race accelerates, it races past us so fast
We are walking ghosts in our own Present,
Dropping off the climbing cliff of If,
Falling off a future that's spinning faster at this moment
Than at any other moment past.
I must to prayer, Daniel, bye. (*Exits.*)

ROTTEN: The prostitution line kind of stung,
But as for all that spinning, bring it on.
I love dizzy. Give me dizzy. Give me Faster Now Than Ever.
You fall backward into kneeling prayer
I fall farther back to pagan grace
And land solidly on ground; then in the ground, where we all end up,
Miss Thing, Six feet deep.

2.9

At a performance of 'The Virtuoso' by Thomas Shadwell. ROBERT HOOKE is there.

WALDORF: I seen this one already. It's pretty good.

STATLER: Don't tell me how it ends.

CHARLES: Relax Roger, theatre should make men gay.

BROGHILL: I will try your Majesty.

ROTTEN and BLACK take the stage.

LONGVIL: (*Played by BLACK.*) Sir Nicholas Gimcrack has invited us to his house to see a cock-lobster dissected and afterwards to dine with him.

BRUCE: (*Played by ROTTEN.*) What kind of man is he? I have heard he has spent twenty years and two thousand pounds in microscopes to find out the nature of eels in vinegar, mites in a cheese, and the blue of plums which he has subtly found out to be living creatures.

LONGVIL: Yes, one who has broken his brains about the Nature of Aire, who has studied these twenty years to find out several kinds of Fleas, And the oceans on the moon, and never cares for understanding mankind.

BRUCE: But may we not have the honor of seeing Sir Nicholas now?

LONGVIL: The truth is, he is within upon some private business.

CROWD: Flogging his lobster.

LONGVIL: He is learning to swim.

BRUCE: Is there any water hereabouts?

LONGVIL: He does not learn to swim in the water, sir.

BRUCE: Not in the water! How then?

LONGVIL: In his laboratory, a wide room where all his instruments and fine knacks are.

Some in the crowd see ROBERT HOOKE is there.

BRUCE: How is this possible?

LONGVIL: He has a frog in a bowl of water, tied with a packthread by the loins, which packthread Sir Nicholas holds in his teeth, lying upon his belly on a table; and as the frog strikes, he strikes.

BRUCE: This is beyond all precedent. He is the most curious coxcomb breathing.

LONGVIL: He is a rare mechanic philosopher.

CROWD: Boo!

LONGVIL: The College indeed refused him. They envied him.

CROWD: OooOOoo.

BRUCE: Were it not possible to see this Experimenter?

Curtain opens and they discover SIR NICHOLAS GIMCRACK, learning to swim. Crowd applauds.

LONGVIL: Admirably well struck! Rarely swum! Incomparable!

BRUCE: This is the rarest fop that ever was heard of.

NICHOLAS: Let me rest a little to respire. It is wonderful to observe the agility of this animal which, with indefatigable activity it rises and keeps almost its whole body upon the surface of this humid element.

STATLER: Meaning water.

WALDORF: I know I've seen it.

LONGVIL: I doubt but your genius will make art equal if not exceed nature, nor will this or any other frog upon the face of the earth outswim you.

NICHOLAS: Nay, I doubt not, sir, in a very little time to become amphibious.

BRUCE: Have you ever tried in the water, sir?

NICHOLAS: No, sir, but I swim most exquisitely on land.

BRUCE: Do you intend to practice in the water, sir?

NICHOLAS: Never sir. I content myself with the speculative part of swimming; I care not for the practice. Knowledge is my ultimate end.

CROWD: Rear end.

The actors and crowd become aware of HOOKE. The laugher is pointed at him.

BRUCE: Sir, I beseech you. What new curiosities have you found out in physic?

NICHOLAS: I did a rare experiment of transferring the blood of a sheep into a madman.

CROWD: Himself!

NICHOLAS: The emittent sheep died under operation, but the recipient madman soon became ovine or sheepish, he bleated perpetually, had wool growing on him in great quantities, and a sheep's tail did soon emerge or arise from his anus or human fundament.

BRUCE: (*Directed sideways at HOOKE.*) Tis an experiment you'll deserve a monument for.

NICHOLAS: Now if you please, we'll retire. I am sorry I cannot perform the dissection of the lobster. My fishmonger has failed me but I assure you it is the most curious of crustaceous animals whatsoever. After dinner we will survey my microscopes, telescopes, thermometers, barometers, pneumatic engines, strenophonial tubes, and the like.

ALL laugh at ROBERT HOOKE. He storms out.

2.10

BOYLE praying. Elsewhere NEWTON removes HOOKE's portrait from the wall.

BOYLE: Abraham's wife, Sarah, bare him no children.
    And Sarah said unto Abraham, behold now,
    The Lord hath restrained me from bearing.
    I pray thee, go in unto my bondswoman.
    And he went unto the bondswoman, and she conceived.
    And the angel of the Lord said unto her, Behold,
    Thou shalt bear a son, and shalt call his name Ishmael.
    And he will be a wild man; his hand will be against every man,
    And every man's hand against him.
    Now when Abraham was ninety and nine years old
    The Lord spoke unto him:
    Sarah thy wife shall have a child. And in her old age, Sarah was blessed,
    And bare Abraham another son.
    And she called the name of her son, Isaac, who grew, and was weaned.
    Then Sarah saw Ishmael mocking.
    Wherefore she said unto Abraham, cast out this bondswoman and her son;
    For the son of this bondswoman shall not be heir with my son, Isaac.

NEWTON slashes HOOKE's portrait. Finis.

Page from Adriano Shaplin's notebook (see page 98)

(put Charles into 2.4)

~~Boyle~~

Hobbes: ~~these~~ ~~I~~ I am more than
abandoned here. ~~this twin~~
~~My one~~ My life's work will
be~~come~~ evidence against
me. Fear, my twin, ~~is here~~
returns

Boyle: I have never brimmed with so
much hate. My voice is ~~horse~~
~~my frighten~~ ~~horse~~. hoarse, My fingers ~~are~~ numb.
~~hurt is~~ I ~~swear I will~~ never stand to
~~my shaking~~ ~~bray here~~ I can never ~~touch~~
~~hurt is~~
~~soo so~~ so this tow I ~~must~~ never feel ~~so way~~
sore ~~can~~
~~this again~~
I banish ~~this~~ feeling hence
I cannot ~~this way~~ feel this way
It murders my joy
It ~~II~~ scars my soul
~~Dea~~ Disappear
Robert
~~Flee~~ Fly